Lecture Notes of the Institute for Computer Sciences, Social Informatics and Telecommunications Engineering   139

Editorial Board

Ozgur Akan
 Middle East Technical University, Ankara, Turkey
Paolo Bellavista
 University of Bologna, Bologna, Italy
Jiannong Cao
 Hong Kong Polytechnic University, Hong Kong, Hong Kong
Falko Dressler
 University of Erlangen, Erlangen, Germany
Domenico Ferrari
 Università Cattolica Piacenza, Piacenza, Italy
Mario Gerla
 UCLA, Los Angels, USA
Hisashi Kobayashi
 Princeton University, Princeton, USA
Sergio Palazzo
 University of Catania, Catania, Italy
Sartaj Sahni
 University of Florida, Florida, USA
Xuemin (Sherman) Shen
 University of Waterloo, Waterloo, Canada
Mircea Stan
 University of Virginia, Charlottesville, USA
Jia Xiaohua
 City University of Hong Kong, Kowloon, Hong Kong
Albert Zomaya
 University of Sydney, Sydney, Australia
Geoffrey Coulson
 Lancaster University, Lancaster, UK

More information about this series at http://www.springer.com/series/8197

Jason J. Jung · Costin Badica
Attila Kiss (Eds.)

Scalable Information Systems

5th International Conference, INFOSCALE 2014
Seoul, South Korea, September 25–26, 2014
Revised Selected Papers

 Springer

Editors
Jason J. Jung
Chung-Ang University
Seoul
Korea, Republic of (South Korea)

Attila Kiss
Eötvös Loránd University
Budapest
Hungary

Costin Badica
University of Craiova
Craiova
Romania

ISSN 1867-8211   ISSN 1867-822X (electronic)
Lecture Notes of the Institute for Computer Sciences, Social Informatics
and Telecommunications Engineering
ISBN 978-3-319-16867-8   ISBN 978-3-319-16868-5 (eBook)
DOI 10.1007/978-3-319-16868-5

Library of Congress Control Number: 2015937351

Springer Cham Heidelberg New York Dordrecht London
© Institute for Computer Sciences, Social Informatics and Telecommunications Engineering 2015
This work is subject to copyright. All rights are reserved by the Publisher, whether the whole or part of the material is concerned, specifically the rights of translation, reprinting, reuse of illustrations, recitation, broadcasting, reproduction on microfilms or in any other physical way, and transmission or information storage and retrieval, electronic adaptation, computer software, or by similar or dissimilar methodology now known or hereafter developed.
The use of general descriptive names, registered names, trademarks, service marks, etc. in this publication does not imply, even in the absence of a specific statement, that such names are exempt from the relevant protective laws and regulations and therefore free for general use.
The publisher, the authors and the editors are safe to assume that the advice and information in this book are believed to be true and accurate at the date of publication. Neither the publisher nor the authors or the editors give a warranty, express or implied, with respect to the material contained herein or for any errors or omissions that may have been made.

Printed on acid-free paper

Springer International Publishing AG Switzerland is part of Springer Science+Business Media
(www.springer.com)

Preface

As data and knowledge volume keep increasing while global means for information dissemination continue to diversify, new methods, modeling paradigms, and structures are needed to efficiently mount scalability requirements. In the recent years, we have seen the proliferation of the use of heterogeneous distributed systems, ranging from simple Networks of Workstations, to highly complex grid computing environments. Such computational paradigms have been preferred due to their reduced costs and inherent scalability, which pose many challenges to scalable systems and applications in terms of information access, storage, and retrieval. Grid computing, P2P technology, data and knowledge bases, distributed information retrieval technology, and networking technology should all converge to address the scalability concern. Furthermore, with the advent of emerging computing architectures (e.g., SMTs, GPUs, and Multicores) the importance of designing techniques explicitly targeting these systems is becoming more and more important. The 5th International Conference on Scalable Information Systems will focus on a wide array of scalability issues and investigate new approaches to tackle problems arising from the ever-growing size and complexity of information of all kinds.

Particularly, in the era of big data, the scalability of information systems has been the most important issue. The aim of this conference is to provide an internationally respected forum for scientific research in the computer-based methods of collective intelligence and their applications in (but not limited to) such fields as Scalable Processing (and Architecture) for Big Data and Scalable Systems and Conceptual Modeling.

December 2014   Jason J. Jung

Organization

InfoScale 2014 is organized by the Department of Computer Science, Chung-Ang University and Wrocław University of Technology in cooperation with The European Alliance for Innovation (EAI).

Executive Committee

General Chair

Jason J. Jung   Chung-Ang University, Korea
Costin Badica   University of Craiova, Romania

Program Chair

Jason J. Jung   Chung-Ang University, Korea
Ngoc Thanh Nguyen   Wrocław University of Technology, Poland
Attila Kiss   Eötvös Loránd University, Hungary

Workshop Chair

David Camacho   Universidad Autónoma de Madrid, Spain

Publicity Chair

Le Anh Vu   Nguyen Tat Thanh University, Vietnam

Publication Chair

Yue-Shan Chang   National Taipei University, Taiwan

Local Chair

Seung-Bo Park   Inha University, Korea

Web Chair

Xuan Hau Pham   Quang Binh University, Vietnam

Conference Coordinator

Sinziana Vieriu   EAI, Italy

Program Committee

G.A. Aranda-Corral   Universidad de Sevilla, Spain
Costin Badica   University of Craiova, Romania
David Camacho   Universidad Autónoma de Madrid, Spain
Yue-Shan Chang   National Taipei University, Taiwan

F. Freitas	Universidade Federal de Pernambuco, Brazil
D. Godoy	UNICEN University, Argentina
T. Herawan	University of Malaya, Malaysia
T.-P. Hong	National University of Kaohsiung, Taiwan
A. Jatowt	Kyoto University, Japan
Jason J. Jung	Chung-Ang University, Korea
K. Juszczyszyn	Wrocław University of Technology, Poland
C. Kartsaklis	Oak Ridge National Laboratory, USA
Attila Kiss	Eötvös Loránd University, Hungary
D. Krol	Wrocław University of Technology, Poland
M. Lanzenberger	Vienna University of Technology, Austria
J. Li	University of Technology, Sydney, Australia
V. Milea	Erasmus University Rotterdam, The Netherlands
G. Nalepa	AGH University of Science and Technology, Poland
T.B. Nguyen	International Institute for Applied Systems Analysis, Austria
Hong-Linh Truong	Vienna University of Technology, Austria
Xinhua Zhu	University of Technology, Sydney, Australia
Michael Sheng	The University of Adelaide, Australia
Tzung-Shi Chen	National University of Tainan, Taiwan
Rajkumar Buyya	University of Melbourne, Australia

Sponsoring Institutions

EAI (European Alliance for Innovation)
Chung-Ang University, Korea
Wrocław University of Technology, Poland

Contents

Scalable Data Analytics

Scalable Similarity Search for Big Data
Challenges and Research Objectives

Pavel Zezula[✉]

Masaryk University, Brno, Czech Republic
zezula@fi.muni.cz

Abstract. Analysis of contemporary Big Data collections require an effective and efficient content-based access to data which is usually unstructured. This first implies a necessity to uncover descriptive knowledge of complex and heterogeneous objects to make them findable. Second, multimodal search structures are needed to efficiently execute complex similarity queries possibly in outsourced environments while preserving privacy. Four specific research objectives to tackle the challenges are outlined and discussed. It is believed that a relevant solution of these problems is necessary for a scalable similarity search operating on Big Data.

Keywords: Big data · Scalability · Information retrieval · Similarity search · Findability · Data outsourcing · Data privacy · Information extraction

1 The Big Data Problem

Many organizations today are increasingly not able to process or analyze data produced by numerous sources. Such situation has given rise to existence of the Big Data problem. In practice, organizations have potential access to a wealth of information, but they do not know how to get value out of it. This is especially true when the prevalently semi-structured or unstructured data is only stored in its raw form. According to [25], the typical characteristic is that the volume of data available to organizations today is on sharp rise, while the percentage of data they can analyze or otherwise selectively use is on decline. In general, it is the *volume*, *variety* and *velocity* of current data which together define the Big Data phenomenon.

Unlike traditional databases, optimized for fast access and summarization of structured data and well defined queries, Big Data is believed to serve as a raw material for the creation of new knowledge. The *big data analytics* is a process of examining large amounts of data of a variety of types to uncover hidden patterns, unknown correlations and other useful information [6]. To allow this, the data needs to be primarily accessed using the similarity of the data content. The white paper [1] of a community of leading researchers across the United States analyzed the problem from the technical point of view. Specifically, they see the heterogeneity, scale, timeliness, complexity, and privacy aspects of Big Data as

© Institute for Computer Sciences, Social Informatics and Telecommunications Engineering 2015
J. Jung et al. (Eds.): INFOSCALE 2014, LNICST 139, pp. 3–12, 2015.
DOI: 10.1007/978-3-319-16868-5_1

the main obstacles of the process that can create value from data. They believe that the problem starts right away during data acquisition, when the massive amounts of data produced require making decisions about what data to keep and what to discard, and how to store the kept data reliably along with proper search enabling meta-data.

Typical examples of the current data are blogs and tweets, which are weakly structured texts, while the more bulky images and video data are only structured for storage and display, but totally unstructured according to semantic content. As it is the content which makes retrieval possible, its extraction into a searchable form is the major challenge. Furthermore, it is necessary to specify how the similarity of data should be evaluated. Contemporary content surrogates (features, descriptors) are only comparable according to specific forms of similarity, which is from the user point of view subjective and context dependent. Accordingly, scalable and secure data analysis, organization, retrieval, and modeling are other foundational technological challenges of Big Data, in general.

Future data processing tools will have to manage the similarity paradigm for searching. Though other alternatives exists, in the following, we will assume the *metric space* model of similarity [23], which has already proved useful mainly for its high extensibility that allows covering a large range of applications by a single search system implementation. The underlying property of any future search related technology is the *scalability*. Then, there are two principle directions in which the future research effort should follow:

– First, it is necessary to concentrate on the problem of data *findability*, which is a general concept that covers technologies for effective and efficient data content acquisition, recording, information extraction and cleaning, as well as the data annotation, integration, and categorization.
– The second direction concerns similarity searching, which is not entirely a new problem, and the future emphasis should be put on efficiency of multi-aspect similarity and on privacy of search in outsourced data environments.

The seemingly independent sub-problems of findability and searching are actually strictly complementary. No search is possible without content-revealing features produced by findability processes on raw data objects. At the same time, unorganized multiple features of objects have little value without multimodal, scalable and secure search mechanisms. These problems are not only timely, but also foundational as they require rethinking of current data processing approaches in fundamental ways. The expectation is to move current search capabilities form processing of small collections to much larger dimensions, from precise to approximate similarity searching, and from using customized infrastructures and services to outsourced processing in secure cloud-like environments. These problems and their relationships are sketched in Fig. 1.

2 Similarity Searching

The ability to perceive similarity is one of the most fundamental aspects of human cognition. Besides being crucial for recognition, classification, and learning, it plays

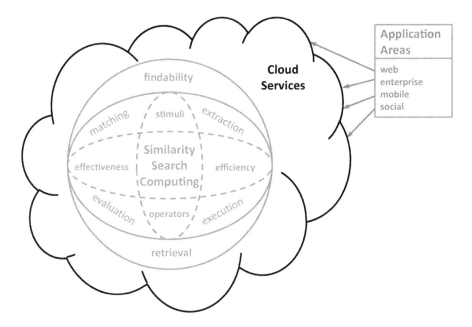

Fig. 1. Similarity search computing services.

an important role in scientific discovery and creativity. In recent years, similarity and analogy have received increasing attention from cognitive scientists [14]. Successful learning mostly depends on the ability to identify the most relevant bodies of knowledge that already exist in memory, so that this knowledge can be used as the starting point for learning something new.

As any kind of fact can nowadays become a digital part of the networked media – whatever we see, say, measure, observe, test, or otherwise experience, is or at least can be in digital form – computers must provide access to required data through operations based on similarity (proximity, resemblance, psychological distance, etc.), because "it is the similarity that is in the world revealing" [21]. There are many application areas that inherently require similarity data management, e.g. multimedia retrieval, processing of biometric data, medical information systems, biology (chemical-)data processing, geographic systems, electronic commerce, forensics, etc. To uncover hidden knowledge in Big Data, similarity access is indispensable.

In the digital world, similarity is determined by stimuli (features, descriptors, properties, etc.) extracted from raw objects and by the way we pursue processes of assessing similarity of related objects, i.e. a sequence of operations from a specific data-processing algebra. We can calibrate the stimuli and operations from two different points of view: (1) *effectiveness* concerns the way similarity is defined, including quality assessment of the results, and (2) *efficiency* regards the processing speed, costs, or the amount of effort needed to get the results – for convenience, see again Fig. 1.

The effectiveness of similarity search necessarily depends on a specific application and data domain. The key tasks are thus the selection of appropriate similarity model and, typically, extraction of convenient feature descriptors obtained from the raw data. In practice, groups of domain experts develop application-specific similarity models and descriptors. For instance, in the domain of images, there exists a wide portfolio of features, ranging from various global descriptors (colors, texture, shapes) and local descriptors (e.g. popular SIFTs) to many domain specific characteristics, such as the face descriptors, and many others. From the application point of view, it is important to select and extract suitable descriptors and effectively combine several types of them.

As far as the efficiency of similarity data management is concerned, it would be very time-consuming and expensive to develop a specialized management system for each of the many application areas and a practically endless list of different similarity criteria applicable on current scale of digital data. Therefore, a lot of research effort has been invested in the last decade into a generic indexing and searching approach that adopts the *metric space* as its data similarity model [23]. This research stream seeks new efficient ways to locate user-relevant information in collections of objects where the relationships are quantified using pair-wise distance (dissimilarity) measures between stimuli of individual objects. So far, many fundamental principles, indexing and searching techniques, implementation paradigms, and analytic tools were developed. Similarity searching in very large data collections is inherently an infrastructure-demanding and time-consuming task, thus many approximate approaches [24] as well as parallel and distributed indexes [18] were also developed. There are also pioneering works that transfer the computationally intensive tasks to new massively parallel hardware infrastructures like GPUs [12]. However, the Big Data problem introduces qualitatively new challenges, in particular the need to process enormous data volumes with respect to multiple complementary views on the complex data similarity.

In summary, though numerous indexing structures has been proposed and used in practice [23], the similarity searching is not ready for Big Data processing. The choice of the most suitable descriptors and the process of their efficient extraction have always been underestimated. Existing retrieval algorithms are able to efficiently process only a single form of similarity and the desired combination of different modalities is typically applied as a posteriori time-consuming process. The data privacy issues which naturally arise in outsourced environments have been considered only marginally in the context of similarity searching. All such deficiencies are even more significant considering the Big Data and form new challenges for research.

3   Challenges and Research Objectives

Seemingly, the Big Data analytics could be done with software tools that are commonly used in advanced analytics disciplines such as predictive analytics and data mining. However, the unstructured data used in Big Data analytics typically do not fit in traditional data warehouses – these tools are often not able to handle the processing demands posed by such data. Current technologies associated with Big Data analytics are therefore based on NoSQL databases and MapReduce-like systems that form the core of an open-source software toolkit for processing large structured data sets across distributed systems. However, new technologies are needed to deal with massive swaths of unstructured, mostly multimedia, data. So the principle two challenges are to:

Challenge 1: bring up descriptive knowledge or content of raw data to increase findability of complex (unstructured) digital data,
Challenge 2: apply such knowledge for efficient multimodal and secure similarity searching in outsourced infrastructure environments.

Accordingly, the principle research directions are: (1) Processing Raw Data for Findability and (2) Hybrid similarity search index structures. In the following, we discuss both of them in more details.

3.1   Processing Raw Data for Object Findability

Indexing and retrieval of multimedia data requires the raw data preprocessed and represented in some structured way. There are two kinds of problems to be considered: what to extract and how to extract. As a large portion of the data currently produced is of no interest (redundant, noisy, or otherwise irrelevant), it can be filtered out and thus compressed by orders of magnitude. However, a big challenge is to find such filters that would not discard useful information; these filters could also serve for profile-specific classification of the data. In a wider context, the objective is to propose theories and techniques that would enable (semi-)automatic feature selection/extraction and classification of unstructured objects stored in heterogeneous Big Data collections. This would allow to automate the arduous task that now has to be done by highly-qualified experts whenever a new collection is to be uploaded to a similarity management system. To achieve this, huge volumes of data have to be processed and complex computational tasks applied which inherently needs sophisticated techniques able to exploit massive cloud-like infrastructures nowadays available. The following two specific objectives concern effectiveness and efficiency of the problem.

Objective 1: Effectives of Findability in Heterogeneous Big Data Collections. After two decades of development, the similarity search technologies only hesitantly find their places in mainstream database management systems. This is mainly because the similarity management does not provide such comfort to end users as, for example, relational databases or web search engines do. The crucial limitation of applicability of current similarity-based systems is the inevitable participation of domain-specific data analysis able to produce a particular similarity model effective for a given data – it also determines the feature extraction processes necessary for retrieval. The role of a domain expert is extremely important and conditions the success of the whole thing. Even if we resort to just image data, we find out that many sub-domains exist, ranging from some more general to a very narrow one. Let us mention a few examples. The architectural images (e.g., pictures of a city) are usually matched locally and the SIFT descriptors work very well here [5], but for general photography the SIFT-like approaches completely fail. In this case, the feature signatures or color descriptors defined by the MPEG7 standard [15] serve better, provided that the distribution of color patches in images is relevant for the user. For cartoons or sketches the shape-based MPEG7 descriptors could be successfully applied [19], while for pictures capturing social events the face descriptor is quite useful (e.g., in the Facebook galleries).

The task of finding an appropriate similarity model becomes even more complex for highly specific domains, e.g. in medical or industrial imagery [3]. In the context of Big Data repositories hosted on cloud infrastructures, where the volumes, heterogeneity and velocity of data uploaded are simply "big", the problem of domain specificity of content gets critical. Without suitable data models, the stored data become not findable, unless an army of domain experts is employed to do the analysis in a manual way. The goal of this task is therefore to establish a framework of algorithms for automatic determination of various domain-specific similarity models. In general, the framework would assume an extensible repository of profile-specific filters that would allow to classify collections or individual objects and select suitable similarity/feature extraction model. Such framework should completely bypass the need for a human domain expert. A simplified analogy can be found in the pattern matching tasks, where a positive response to a particular pattern results in classifying an object by the class associated with the pattern. However, in context of similarity models, the "pattern matching idea" is much more complicated as the framework must cope with additional issues, such as the very large volumes of data, large heterogeneity of data (e.g., mixed social and architectural pictures), user preferences, social-networking context, privacy (encrypted data), and many others.

Objective 2: Scalable Content Extraction in Big Data Collections. In order to increase findability of objects a user-specified workload must be applied on every piece of the data. The workload can be of various natures, ranging from feature extraction from complex data to exhaustive information searching or filtering. We can consider the data as a continuously transmitted stream delivered to the processing infrastructure. Specific examples include: extraction of visual descriptors from a large collection of images stored on a disk; classification (annotation) of images for a specific social network user; event detection in a video stream produced by a surveillance camera; re-ranking of outputs from a text search by different similarity metrics, etc.

According to [16], current tools and systems for distributed processing are typically designed either for (1) batch processing of a large data volume that is already stored in a distributed hardware infrastructure (Hadoop-like systems based on the MapReduce processing model), or for (2) parallel and distributed processing of a given complex computational task (systems like Storm or S4). Neither of these approaches is fully sufficient for our problem, since the desired system must cover both these tasks at the same time. Moreover, we need to deal with scenarios when a large bulk of data, stored at one point, must be processed efficiently and stored in a distributed way for further processing; also, results from a stream data processing may need to be merged with previous batch processing results. The intention of this objective is to formalize the described problem and develop a system based on an improved version of the recently proposed lambda architecture [16].

The resulting solution should be able to efficiently process huge heterogeneous data-sets, effectively combining the batch and stream data processing and supporting all the above-mentioned scenarios. The system should be distributed but based on commodity hardware to minimize infrastructure costs. It should allow processing heterogeneous data sources by user-defined computational tasks, thus providing support for the demanding processes with the objective to increase data findability of Big Data collections. Possibilities of applying massively parallel accelerators such as GPUs or Intel Xeon Phi cards in addition to distributed processing should also be considered. These accelerators can be used to offload computationally expensive tasks from regular CPUs thus increase the overall throughput of the system.

3.2   Hybrid Similarity Search Index Structures

It is obvious that a single type of similarity view of complex objects is typically not sufficient for answering different user requests and the situation is getting worse with the increasing size of searched collections. Multiple search criteria usually improve the situation, but complex (combined) similarity search is not very scalable, that is, not projecting well into the space of big data. Specifically, when each similarity measure is indexed by an independent search structure and the Fagin's A0 Algorithm or the Threshold Algorithm [7] are applied as a post-processing step, there is no general upper-bound on access costs.

In order to avoid the costly posteriori combination of index search outcomes, we need a hybrid structure able to index and search multiple similarity types at one time. Basically, the similarity search indexes are based on one of the following implementation principles. The first applies the inverted file paradigm – enormously successful for the *cosine similarity* in vector-space models for text-based searching [2]. The second approach applies multidimensional or metric search structures [20], which are applicable for lower-dimensional spatial queries or generic metric distances. The desired multimodal retrieval structure should embrace both of these principles and allow to conveniently use the inverted file or metric partitioning strategies. Application of such approach would support execution of queries such as: text search constrained by specific geographic locations (e.g. pizza restaurants close to the current GPS location); image similarity search by visual feature descriptors combined with "topic closeness" characterized by keywords attached to each image; visual image search realized by global descriptors (color, texture, shapes) containing a specific detail determined by a set of visual words originating from local SIFT descriptors (e.g. a picture of a football match with the IBM logo advertisement).

Another important problem in the area of indexing structures is to study a secure similarity search in outsourced environments. With the growing volume of data, a natural trend is to outsource the data to other parties that would professionally manage the data and provide the similarity search as a service. However, this principle fundamentally assumes that the data is provided to the third-party shared repositories not fully controlled by the data owner. But, in many cases, the outsourced data may be sensitive (e.g. medical data), confidential, or otherwise valuable (e.g. data collected from a scientific research) and thus the privacy of data is of high importance. Hence, besides providing effective and efficient searching, the future outsourced searching [10,11] should also meet data owner's privacy requirements not only by standard access permissions, but, equally important, by securing the content of the indexed data in a potentially hostile third-party environment. The requirement for encrypted data searched in a multi-modal way results in the following two research objectives.

Objective 3: Multimodal Similarity Searching. In just a few years, geographic web search with spatial-keyword queries has emerged from a niche service to one of the most popular applications. Geo-textual queries are being supported in Google Maps where points of interest can be retrieved, Foursquare where geo-tagged documents can be determined, and Twitter where tweets can be extracted. Spatial-keyword querying is also receiving increasing interest in the research community where a range of techniques have been proposed for its efficient processing [4]. Geo-textual indices usually combine a spatial index and a text index structure. According to the spatial index they utilize, we can distinguish R-tree based indices, Grid-based indices, and Space-filling curve indices. The text indices are primarily based on the inverted file principle. Some geo-textual indices loosely combine a spatial and a textual index while other indices integrate them tightly, resulting in a hybrid index structure.

The similarity search should capitalize on this experience and generalize the idea of geo-textual indices. In fact, the geographic (spatial) dimension could be substituted by an arbitrary metric-space model of similarity, whereas the textual dimension would be extended to support any data and similarity measure for which the inverted file indexing is applicable – e.g. text words, visual words, motion words, etc. The proposed solution would significantly extend the original geographic web search to many, primarily multimedia, new applications, considering the geographic web search as its special case.

Objective 4: Privacy-Preserving Searching. In the context of traditional databases, mostly relational, a lot of attention has recently been focused on the so-called *symmetric searchable encryption schemes* that can form basic building blocks of privacy-preserving outsourced storages. Such schemes allow data owners to encrypt the data in such a way that it is possible to perform selective data retrieval (search) over these encrypted collections [8,9]. Development of encrypted and searchable schemes for generic similarity search is a new and inherently more complicated task with a few very recent pioneering works [10,11,13,22]. Trying to capture the problem in its full complexity requires to focus on the development of technologies and protocols necessary for a client-server similarity-search system with the following properties:

Usability: The solution should be applicable on generic data model, such as the metric space, and should inherently be dynamic, i.e. efficiently supporting both the search and update operations.

Security: Data is stored on the server side in an encrypted form, so that any adversary including the 3rd party cloud provider can learn as little information about the outsourced data as possible. The resistance of the scheme should be evaluated in context of standard attack scenarios [17].

Efficiency: The schemes have to be applicable on large data collections and their efficiency should be considered in context of the client-server architecture, i.e. shifting computational burden to the server side with a minimum communication costs. The update operations should also be efficient.

Current state of the research does not provide solutions for such complex requirements, which opens a large research area with a high practical potential.

4   Conclusions

Similarity search has already proved useful mainly for the text based retrieval, even on the level of the web scale. However, in order to deal with the variety, volume, and the speed of Big Data, several challenging problems are to be solved. In this paper, we have identified four specific objectives, contributing to the solution of two basic similarity management challenges, i.e. the findability and search. Naturally, all possible proposals will have to undergo serious prove of concept verifications by implementing prototypes and testing their properties on representative data-sets, varying the workload as well as power of computational infrastructure. Experience learned from experiments will be vital for a possible future application. To this aim, large and representative data collections are needed – serious benchmark platforms need to be developed.

Acknowledgments. This research was supported by the Czech Science Foundation project number P103/12/G084.

References

1. Challenges and Opportunities with Big Data. A community white paper developed by leading researchers across the United States (2014). http://cra.org/ccc/docs/init/bigdatawhitepaper.pdf. Accessed March 2014

2. Baeza-Yates, R.A., Ribeiro-Neto, B.A.: Modern Information Retrieval - The Concepts and Technology Behind Search. Addison-Wesley, Reading (2011)

3. Beecks, C., Ivanescu, A.M., Seidl, T., Martin, D., Pischke, P., Kneer, R.: Applying similarity search for the investigation of the fuel injection process. In: Ferro, A. (ed.) SISAP, pp. 117–118. ACM (2011)

4. Chen, L., Cong, G., Jensen, C.S., Wu, D.: Spatial keyword query processing: an experimental evaluation. PVLDB **6**(3), 217–228 (2013)

5. Chum, O., Matas, J.: Large-scale discovery of spatially related images. IEEE Trans. Pattern Anal. Mach. Intell. **32**(2), 371–377 (2010)

6. Dhar, V.: Data science and prediction. Commun. ACM **56**(12), 64–73 (2013)
7. Fagin, R., Kumar, R., Sivakumar, D.: Comparing top k lists. In: Proceedings of the Fourteenth Annual ACM-SIAM Symposium on Discrete Algorithms, SODA 2003, pp. 28–36. Society for Industrial and Applied Mathematics, Philadelphia (2003). http://portal.acm.org/citation.cfmid=644108.644113
8. Kamara, S., Charalampos, P., Tom, R.: Dynamic searchable symmetric encryption. In: Proceedings of the 2012 ACM Conference on Computer and Communications Security, pp. 965–976 (2012)
9. Kamara, S., Lauter, K.: Cryptographic cloud storage. In: Sion, R., Curtmola, R., Dietrich, S., Kiayias, A., Miret, J.M., Sako, K., Sebé, F. (eds.) RLCPS, WECSR, and WLC 2010. LNCS, vol. 6054, pp. 136–149. Springer, Heidelberg (2010)
10. Kozak, S.: Efficiency and security in similarity cloud services. PVLDB **6**(12), 1450–1455 (2013)
11. Kozak, S., Novak, D., Zezula, P.: Secure metric-based index for similarity cloud. In: Jonker, W., Petković, M. (eds.) SDM 2012. LNCS, vol. 7482, pp. 130–147. Springer, Heidelberg (2012)
12. Krulis, M., Skopal, T., Lokoc, J., Beecks, C.: Combining CPU and GPU architectures for fast similarity search. Distrib. Parallel Databases **30**(3), 179–207 (2012)
13. Kuzu, M., Islam, M.S., Kantarcioglu, M.: Efficient similarity search over encrypted data. In: Kementsietsidis, A., Salles, M.A.V. (eds.) ICDE. IEEE Computer Society, pp. 1156–1167 (2012)
14. Larkey, L., Markman, A.: Processes of similarity judgment. Cogn. Sci. **29**, 1061–1076 (2005)
15. Lokoč, J., Novák, D., Batko, M., Skopal, T.: Visual image search: feature signatures or/and global descriptors. In: Navarro, G., Pestov, V. (eds.) SISAP 2012. LNCS, vol. 7404, pp. 177–191. Springer, Heidelberg (2012)
16. Marz, N., Warren, J.: Principles and Best Practices of Scalable Realtime Data Systems. Manning Publications Co., Shelter Island (2014)
17. Menezez, A., van Oorschot, P., Vanstone, S.: Handbook of Applied Cryptography. CRR Press, Boca Raton (1997)
18. Novak, D., Batko, M., Zezula, P.: Large-scale similarity data management with distributed metric index. Inf. Process. Manage. **48**(5), 855–872 (2012)
19. Salembier, P., Smith, J.: Overview of MPEG-7 multimedia description schemes and schema tools. In: Introduction to MPEG-7: Multimedia Content Description Interface (2002)
20. Samet, H.: Foundations Of Multidimensional And Metric Data Structures. (Computer Graphics and Geometric Modeling. Morgan Kaufmann Publishers Inc., San Francisco (2005)
21. Vosniadou, S., Ortony, A.: Similarity and Analogical Reasoning. Advances in Database Systems. Cambridge University Press, New York (2003)
22. Yiu, M.L., Assent, I., Jensen, C.S., Kalnis, P.: Outsourced similarity search on metric data assets. IEEE Trans. Knowl. Data Eng. **24**(2), 338–352 (2012)
23. Zezula, P., Amato, G., Dohnal, V., Batko, M.: Similarity Search: The Metric Space Approach. Advances in Database Systems, vol. 32. Springer, New York (2006)
24. Zezula, P., Savino, P., Amato, G., Rabitti, F.: Approximate similarity retrieval with M-trees. VLDB J. **7**(4), 275–293 (1998)
25. Zikopoulos, P., Eaton, C.: Understanding Big Data: Analytics for Enterprise Class Hadoop and Streaming Data. McGraw-Hill Education, New York (2006)

Content-Based Analytics of Diffusion on Social Big Data: A Case Study on Korean Telecommunication Companies

Namhee Lee and Jason J. Jung[(⊠)]

Department of Computer Engineering, Chung-Ang University,
Seoul 156-756, South Korea
j2jung@gmail.com

Abstract. Social networking services have been playing an important role of communicating with customers. Particularly, firms seek to deploy Twitter for the benefit of their business because it has rapidly become an information vehicle for consumers who are disseminating information on products and services. Thus, this study examines how information shared by firms is diffused and what the important factors in understanding information dissemination are. Specially, this study classifies the types of tweets posted by a firm (@olleh_mobile) and then to investigate the effect of these types of tweets on diffusion. By using content analysis, this study defined two categories ('Information providing' and 'Advertisement' type) and eight subordinate concepts (News, Usage, Preview, Notice, Sale, Benefit, Event, Service public relations). These results indicate that the differences are significant for all three types of information content. It shows that firms can spread information more quickly by providing the 'Information and advertisement' type rather than the 'Advertisement' type.

Keywords: Information contents · Information diffusion · Information types · Twitter · Content-based analytics

1 Introduction

Social media and communications technology have become important drivers for new types of communication and have made users better able to share information (Smith 2010). New communication channels and mechanisms like Facebook, Twitter and Wikis, allow the creation and exchange of content that has been created by users and provide collaborative structures where user interaction is proactively encouraged (Kaplan and Haenlein 2010). New media and communication platforms make it easier to spread information very quickly and make one person able to communicate with hundreds or thousands of others.

One well known social media channel, Twitter, is a short message service. It has attracted advertising and marketing interest from firms to improve brand trust and loyalty for customers (Sledgianowski and Kulviwat 2009). Twitter allows firms to engage in timely and direct end-user contact at relatively low cost and higher levels of efficiency than can be achieved with more traditional communication tools (Kaplan and

© Institute for Computer Sciences, Social Informatics and Telecommunications Engineering 2015
J. Jung et al. (Eds.): INFOSCALE 2014, LNICST 139, pp. 13–27, 2015.
DOI: 10.1007/978-3-319-16868-5_2

Haenlein 2010). Therefore firms cannot ignore the importance of Twitter because it has rapidly become an information vehicle for consumers who are disseminating information on products and services (Fischer and Reuber 2011).

As a growing number of firms seek to deploy Twitter for the benefit of their business, the current study extends investigations that consider how companies use Twitter to facilitate dialogic communication with their consumers (Greer and Ferguson 2011; Jansen et al. 2009; Li and Rao 2010). Even though there are various discussions about how information can be disseminated on Twitter, most research topics on Twitter are related to personal, social or public news (Cha et al. 2010; Li and Rao 2010). This scope of this study is the type of determinants influencing information diffusion for firms which use Twitter. Thus, in spite of the growth of Twitter, the business viability of Twitter remains in question. Also, managers within firms are still uncertain as to how Twitter can be used in marketing and which types of message exert the most influence or get reposted by users (Kim et al. 2012).

Therefore, this study examines how information shared by firms is diffused and what the important factors in understanding information dissemination are. More specifically, this study poses the research questions: (1) What types of information are provided by a firm using Twitter? (2) How does the diffusion of information that is posted by a firm differ by different types of information? Through these questions, this study will suggest content that is appropriate for diffusion and the relationship between patterns of tweets and diffusion on Twitter. It is expected that there can be a significant impact derived from analysis of information diffusion to guide firms Twitter use.

The remainder of this study is structured as follows. In the next section, we present the theoretical background and develop the research framework. This is followed by a description of the methods employed, including the data, variable operationalization, and analysis techniques. Finally, this study presents results, and ends with a discussion of limitations and theoretical and practical implications of the findings.

2 Theoretical Background

2.1 Understanding Twitter

Twitter is an online social networking and micro-blogging service. It is a social networking service because users have a profile page and connect to other users by following them (Thelwall et al. 2011). Also, Twitter offers a micro-blogging service by allowing its users to send messages- called "tweets" – to their followers while visiting other users' accounts (Savage 2011). Tweets are text-based posts of up to 140 characters in length. On Twitter, users can post original tweets under their Twitter accounts and can "Retweet", which means posting another user's tweet. When a person chooses to follow someone, they receive their tweets (Fischer and Reuber 2011). The purpose of retweeting is to diffuse information to followers, and this diffusion seems to be extremely rapid (Thelwall et al. 2011). Therefore, retweeting is the key mechanism for information diffusion in Twitter.

2.2   Previous Research of Twitter Usage by Business

Many firms use Twitter as a marketing tool. Twitter is useful to disseminate information or messages related to their products or service to customers. A number of firms use Twitter to disseminate information to stakeholders (Jansen et al. 2009). Also, Twitter gives business an opportunity to track what consumers are saying about their products and allow consumers to post instant opinions about a certain brand even though not have any previous relationship (Savage 2011). According to a recent report, 103 Chief Marketing Officers responded to the question asking which platform would figure into their marketing plans the most in the coming months. 40.8 % responded Twitter, followed by 26.2 % saying Facebook, 16.5 % saying LinkedIn, and 8.7 % responding "Other". For example, Dell Outlet used Twitter to reach consumers and found out that consumers were interested in communicating via Twitter.

Research of business usage of Twitter is at a very early stage of development (Barnes and BöHringer 2011). Zhang and Watts (2008), Jansen et al. (2009), and Berinato (2010) showed how to use Twitter for promotion and branding in firms. In these studies, Twitter is described as a tool to create communication with consumers. While previous work on Twitter has been extensive, it has generally focused only on single perspectives or factors for using Twitter.

2.3   The Diffusion of Innovations Theory

Diffusion theory has been studied in a variety of contexts and from many perspectives. The Rogers model provides a reasonably comprehensive view of innovation diffusion (Brancheau and Wetherbe 1990). Since the publication of Rogers's widely referenced work, the diffusion model's focus on the individual adoption process and emphasis on communication behavior have been extended to technology and information adoption (Bajwa et al. 2008; Chatman 1986).

Rogers (1983) defines diffusion to be "the process by which an innovation is communicated through certain channels over time among the members of a social systems". So diffusion is a special type of communication in which the messages are about new ideas (Rogers 2003). Innovation, as an idea or object, is a key factor in diffusion theory. The characteristics of innovation are one important explanation of diffusion. Rogers and Shoemaker (1971) identify the most important innovation characteristics that influence the adoption of an innovation as trialability, relative advantage, compatibility, observability, and complexity. Previous studies have considered innovation or information characteristics such as usefulness, accuracy, and source or credibility (Cheung et al. 2008). These characteristics influence the diffusion of innovations or information about new ideas.

Thus, the diffusion approach helps to understand how individuals behave as they consider the adoption of an innovation. Moreover, it is a useful theory to know the diffusion process in online communities. The characteristics of information or messages in social networking may play a special role in diffusion (Zhao and Rosson 2009). However, research on diffusion has concentrated primarily on innovation and its characteristics (Chatman 1986). Research perspectives are limited to understanding the diffusion patterns of information.

3 Research Model and Hypotheses

Based on classical diffusion of innovation theory, this study developed a research model as shown in Fig. 1. Consistent with this purpose of this study, information content in tweets provided by firms are classified into three types. The model examines the effect of patterns of information content on three attributes of information diffusion (scale, speed and duration).

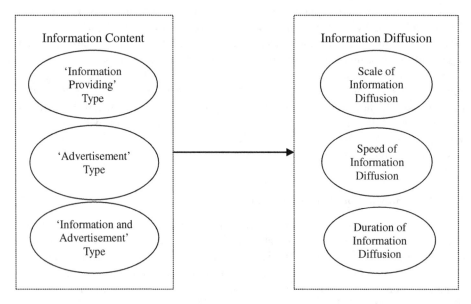

Fig. 1. The conceptual research model

Information characteristics influence a user's decision to spread information. Individual perceptions of the attributes of information can affect its rate of adoption (Rogers 1983; Rogers 2003), Chatman (1986) suggests that the phenomenon of diffusion can shift from information characteristics or contents. For example, information about a job can be circulated quickly because this type of information is time-sensitive. Most studies focus on characteristics of innovation and information such as usefulness, message relevance, accuracy, comprehensiveness (Cheung et al. 2008). It measures how users perceive these characteristics as related to its value, and in relationship to their past experience (Rogers 2003).

Even on Twitter, the types of information tweets suggest is important to diffusion. Tweets can be categorized based on many types of content. Java et al. (2007) identify tweets' contents with reference to information sharing, information seeking, and relationships. Naaman et al. (2010) suggest nine content categories including information sharing, opinion, complaint, self-promotion etc. The characteristics of messages shared on Twitter may play a special role in sharing or delivering information (Zhao and Rosson 2009). Consequently, information diffusion will depend on the type of content.

Hypothesis 1
  The content of information will have a significant effect on information diffusion.
Hypothesis 1a
  The content of information will have a significant effect on the scale of information diffusion.
Hypothesis 1b
  The content of information will have a significant effect on the speed of information diffusion.
Hypothesis 1c
  The content of information will have a significant effect on the duration of information diffusion.

4 Research Methodology

This study was conducted to test the proposed model for information diffusion on Twitter. The research model was applied to the content and type of information in tweets created by a firm. A content analysis of tweets was performed using coding messages. Then a cluster and non-parametric ANOVA analysis was conducted to determine the types of information content that influence diffusion.

4.1 Data Collection

As the study's objectives are first to classify the types of tweets posted by a firm and then to investigate the effect of these types of tweets on diffusion, an in-depth perspective such as that offered by the Twitter experiences of a particular firm was deemed appropriate. In order to collect a realistic Twitter dataset, this study used a commercial system (called TweetScope). This system can manage tweet streams from multi-user accounts simultaneously in real-time. Using TwitterScope, 1006 tweets posted by the @olleh_mobile account, from March 16th, 2012 to October 11th, 2012 were downloaded. The Olleh_mobile business has been actively interested in Twitter to promote the brand. It has 116,376 followers, 496 followings and 105,414 tweets. Olleh_mobile has posted a total of 104,824 tweets and 25 tweets daily on average. The data includes the content of tweets, tweet time, and the number of retweets (RTs). Also, this data contains information on users who repost tweets, user ID, times of users' RT, the number of followers, followings, and total tweets. Excluded were mention tweets because these are not delivered automatically to followers. This study analyzed 1006 tweets.

4.2 Measure

4.2.1 Dependent Variables: Information Diffusion

In Rogers (1983) model, diffusion was defined as how many people use or adopt new ideas, or technology and measured the cumulative number of adopters. Previous studies measured diffusion by means of dependent variables such as binary adoption/non-adoption, time of adoption, and frequency of use (Fichman 1992).

Table 1. Dependent variables definitions

Variables	Definition	Measure	Reference
The scale of RTs	How many times a tweet is reposted by users	The number of RTs	Cheung et al. (2008)
The speed of RTs	How fast a tweet is reposted by users	Total RTs (n)/Starting time of RT – Ending time of RT (hour)	Yang and Counts (2010)
The duration of RTs	How long a tweet is reposted by users	The gap between Starting time of RT and Ending time of RT (hour)	

Similarly, on Twitter, diffusion means how much or far tweet propagates throughout the community of users or followers. Diffusion is generally measured as the number of retweets – these are posted tweets sent to followers on Twitter. Yang and Counts (2010) developed three dimensions of diffusion: speed, scale and range. In this study, information diffusion is measured by three dimensions, as shown in Table 1.

4.2.2   Independent Variables: Information Contents

4.2.2.1 Coding Framework and Procedure

This study used content analysis by first conceptualizing the content of tweetsto characterize the rationale for tweets posted by a firm on Twitter. Recently, as research about social media has increased, much of it focuses on the purpose of information or communication and also on new communication behaviors (Herring et al. 2004; Papacharissi 2004). This research uses content analysis. This analysis was conducted to identify and quantify structural factors or properties of websites, blogs and social network sites (Ha and E.L. James 1998; Lin and Pena 2011).

Content analysis is considered to be a qualitative research method. It is effective in examining both theoretical definitions and empirical measurements. This analysis provides researchers with opportunities to unobtrusively study the values, sentiments, intentions and ideologies of sources generally inaccessible to researchers (Morris 1994). The goal of content analysis is to create objective criteria for transforming written text contained in highly reliable data (Simmons et al. 2011). It classifies content analysis methods into three types: (1) human-scored schema, (2) individual word count systems, and (3) computerized systems using artificial intelligence. Content analysis may provide an effective tool for gaining access to desired study information.

In this study, to analyze the content of tweets, two coders independently looked through downloaded tweets and classified the purpose of tweets based on previous studies and theories. Then the study compared and contrasted each classification deduced by coders.

In this step, while two coders agree on representations for three types of content and different types of subordinate categories, while also agreeing on the elimination of inappropriate concepts. Finally, tweets provided by a firm were classified into two categories (information providing and advertisement) and eight subordinate content

Table 2. The level of agreement in information content

Constructs	Variables		The level of agreement	N
Information contents	Information providing	News	86 %	58
		Usage	93 %	336
		Review	97 %	225
		Notice	84 %	145
	Advertisement	Sale	85 %	29
		Benefit	89 %	199
		Event	92 %	159
		Service public relations	92 %	46

groupings (News, Usage, Review, Notice, Sale, Benefit, Event, Service PR) as shown below in Table 2.

Two coders received training and analyzed the tweets according to the predetermined categories. Each coder had the chance to practice the procedure with a few examples before the actual coding started. A tweet could be classified into more than one category. For example, a tweet that provides information could also express advertisement. Overall intercoder reliability, as measured by their performance on the total set of tweets, was assessed by using Cohen's kappa. Cohen's kappa is a more rigorous means of assessing reliability than using other statistics such as an exact percent agreement because it accounts for chance when measuring the level of agreement between two coders (Boettger and Palmer 2010). For this study the kappa test identified an overall agreement of above 80 %, indicating an acceptable level of consistency between coders.

4.3 Types of Information in Firm's Twitter Messages

A few researches looked at objectives of social media by using content analysis. Fullwood et al. (2009) categorize the purpose of blogs into categories diary, advertising, providing information, sharing media, emotional outlet, and reporting. Naaman et al. (2010) developed a content-based categorization of messages posted by Twitter users. They suggested nine message categories: information sharing, self promotion, opinion, statements, and questions to followers, presence maintenance, and anecdotes. Furthermore, Java et al. (2007) identified four user objectives on Twitter, daily chatter, conversations, sharing information and reporting news.

Based on the knowledge gained from these studies, this study defined two categories and eight subordinate concepts. First, the 'Information providing' type contains data, information or knowledge concerning a firm's activities, service usage, notice and review. Second, 'Advertisement' type suggests the price or brand name for users to purchase or use a product or service. Also this type contains the messages which make

Table 3. Examples of each type of information content

Variables		Definition	Keywords
Information providing	News	Reporting current activities about a firm	Current, partnership, interview
	Usage	Information on how to use service	Procedure, pay method, explain
	Review	Evaluating service or product improvements	Compare, review, postscript
	Notice	Introducing new products and giving announcements of a play, concert or special happening	Announce, launch, release
Advertisement	Sale	Suggesting price of products	Purchase, price
	Benefit	Suggesting use and benefit information about products	Discount, free, low price, compensation
	Event	Leading consumers to participate in events	Participation, event
	Public relations	Publicity concerning services or events	Event recommendations

users participate in events related to the product. Table 3 shows examples of each type of information content.

4.4   Analysis and Results

4.4.1   The Description of Information Contents

The intent was to examine whether olleh_mobile employed different tweets across the diffusion of tweets. This study considered two super-ordinate categories and eight sub-concepts. Of 886 tweets created by the olleh_mobile firm, "Information providing" tweets were about 64 % and "Advertisement" tweets were about 36 %. Results related to the four categories were 1) "Information providing" (News 5 %, Usage 28 %, Review 19 %, Notice 12 %) and the other four categories were in 2) "Advertisement" (Sale 2 %, Benefit 17 %, Event 13 %, PR 4 %). The results show that theolleh_mobile firm usually uses Twitter for informing customers about how to use products and services, and review of products and services.

Using the above characterization of tweet contents, this study determined whether differences in content appeared across the diffusion dimensions. Table 4 represents the results analysis of information diffusion according to information contents. The scale of RTs in "Information providing" type was news (6.52), usage (6.10), review (6.50) and notice (7.80). The speed of RTs in "Information providing" type was news (2.58), usage (19.20), review (16.20) and notice (15.60). The duration of RTs in "Information providing" type was news (30.50), usage (29.50), review (7.90) and notice (40.10). Also, the scale of RTs in "Advertisement" type was sale (4.80), benefit (18.40), event

Table 4. Information diffusion of information content

Constructs	Variables		Scale	Speed	Duration	N
Information content	Information providing	News	6.52	2.58	30.50	58
		Usage	6.10	19.20	29.50	336
		Review	6.50	16.20	7.90	225
		Notice	7.80	15.60	40.10	145
	Advertisement	Sale	4.80	1.20	13.20	29
		Benefit	18.40	3.00	62.10	199
		Event	21.50	1.02	74.40	159
		Service PR	7.10	1.56	31.98	46

(21.50), and service PR (7.10). The speed of RTs in "Advertisement" type was sale (1.20), benefit (3.00), event (1.02), and service PR (1.56). The duration of RTs in "Advertisement" type was sale (13.20), benefit (62.10), event (74.40), and service PR (31.98).

Findings indicated that Event and Benefit variables had the highest score occurring on the scale of RTs (21.50, 18.40) and duration of RTs (74.40, 62.10). The Usage variable had the highest score with respect to the speed of RTs. These results suggest that the advertisement type of tweets is more spread-out and the information type of tweets is shared most quickly. In addition, the result relating to the duration of RTs suggests that tweets or content do not last long. They remained an average of two days on Twitter.

4.5   The Impact of Information Contents on Diffusion

The first goal of this model was to evaluate whether there is a difference between information content related to information diffusion. Hypothesis H1 says that "The content types of information will have a significant effect on three types of information diffusion". To examine this hypothesis, this study examined groupings across types of tweets by using cluster analysis which is typically utilized to examine patterns in various categories (Segars and Grover 1999).

This analysis separates data into groups that are represented by clusters, which can be meaningful, useful, or both. The clusters are constructed to be as internally homogenous as possible while also being as externally heterogeneous as possible. Numerous clustering algorithms have been used for the analysis of quantitative and qualitative data, and interested readers are encouraged to read the review of data clustering (Miaskiewicz and Monarchi 2008). Although several clustering algorithms exist, Ward's minimum variance criterion was chosen for this analysis (Punj and Stewart 1983). The clustering criterion of this technique is minimization of total within-group sums of squares (Segars and Grover 1999).

The result of this analysis shows a three-cluster solution. Three clusters that emerged from the analysis were identified "Advertisement" (Benefit and Event),

Table 5. Description of information content clusters (means and standard deviation)

Variables	Cluster 1 (N = 189) "AD type"		Cluster 2 (N = 323) "IF type"		Cluster 3 (N = 374) "IF_AD type"	
	Mean	S.D.	Mean	S.D.	Mean	S.D.
Scale of RTs	19.28	29.43	4.01	5.06	5.96	6.56
Speed of RTs	1.16	2.45	19.70	171.14	15.76	125.32
Duration of RTs	66.50	133.87	27.02	97.37	13.80	53.43

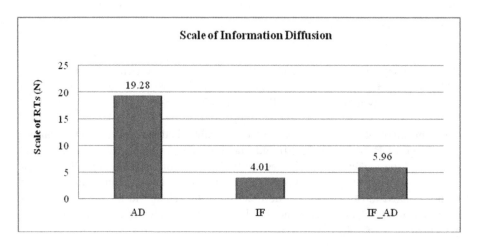

Fig. 2. The scale of information diffusion in three clusters

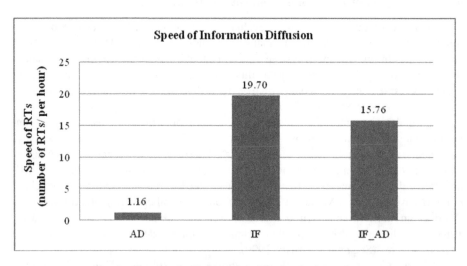

Fig. 3. The speed of information diffusion in three clusters

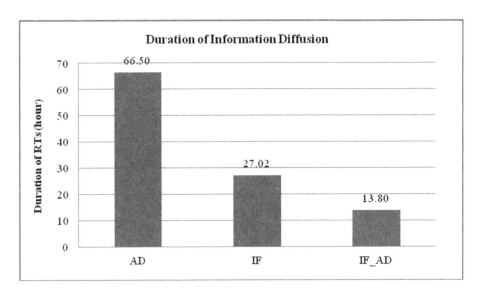

Fig. 4. The duration of information diffusion in three clusters

"Information providing" (Usage) and "Information and Advertisement" (Sale, Service PR, News, Review, Notice) as shown the Table 5.

The 189 tweets identified as "Advertisement" type are characterized by average scores on the scale of RTs, speed of RTs and duration of RTs. These results indicate that the scale (M = 19.28) and duration (M = 66.50) of RTs in this cluster are higher than other clusters. Also, the "Information" type cluster includes 323 tweets. This type has allow scale of RTs (M = 4.01). However, the speed of RTs (M = 19.70) is the highest score among three types of tweets. The cluster labeled "Information and Advertisement" consists of 374 tweets that show the lowest duration of RTs (M = 13.80). These results show that the "Advertisement" type is more associated with the scale and duration of RTs and "Information providing" type is more linked to the speed of RTs. Figures 2, 3 and 4 show the result of information diffusion according to information clusters.

After clusters of information contents were identified, a non-parametric test, the Kruskal-Wallis test was employed to explore the existence of diffusion differences. Within this study, differences between clusters are examined across the three dimensions of information diffusion. The Kruskal Wallis one-way analysis of variance by ranks does not assume a normal distribution, the analogous one-way analysis of variance. It is advantageous in statistical analysis to use ranks. The only assumptions underlying the use of ranks made are that the observations are all independent, that all those within a given sample come from a single population, and that the C populations are of approximately the same form (Kruskal and Wallis 1957). The test statistics are described by the following equation

$$W = \left[\frac{12}{N(N+1)} \sum_{i=1}^{k} \frac{R^2}{n_i}\right] - 3(N+1)$$

where k indicates the number of samples, and n_i and R_i mean the numbers of the observations and ranks in the ith sample, respectively.

Table 6 describes the summary statistics and correlation. Tables 7 and 8 suggest that the three-cluster solution represents meaningful differences in information content across the sampled firm. Table 8 outlines the results of the Kruskal-Wallis test for differences in information content across each dimension of information diffusion. These results indicate that the differences are significant for all three types of information content (Scale of RTs $p < .001$, Speed of RTs $p < .001$ and Duration of RTs $p < .001$). These findings provide support for hypothesis H1.

Table 6. Summary statistics and correlation matrix

	Mean	S.D	1	2	3	4	5	6
1. Scale of RTs	8.90	15.69	1.000					
2. Duration of RTs	29.86	97.45	.710**	1.000				
3. Speed of RTs	14.08	131.62	.511**	.129**	1.000			
4. IF_AD	1.09	1.45	−.218**	−.062	−.175**	1.000		
5. IF	0.84	0.99	.040	−.169**	.219**	−.647**	1.000	
6. AD	0.21	0.41	.208**	.277**	−.059	−.394**	−.445**	1.000

Table 7. Rank of Kruskal-Wallis test

	Cluster	N	Mean rank
Scale of RTs	Advertisement	189	545.10
	Information providing	374	455.56
	Information_Advertisement	323	370.09
	Total	886	
Duration of RTs	Advertisement	189	578.56
	Information providing	374	393.34
	Information_Advertisement	323	422.56
	Total	886	
Speed of RTs	Advertisement	189	415.51
	Information providing	374	508.58
	Information_Advertisement	323	384.52
	Total	886	

Table 8. Result of Kruskal-Wallis test

	Scale of RTs	Speed of RTs	Duration of RTs
Chi Square	57.769	44.173	70.054
DF	2	2	2
P value	.000	.000	.000

Note. **p < .05 ***p < .01

5   Conclusions

This study proposed an integrated research model based on diffusion of innovations and two-step flow theory. It classified information content and examined the effect of information content on diffusion of information. This study includes a number of theoretical implications. Previous studies focused on the characteristics of information within limited scopes (Rogers 1983; Rogers 2003). This study arrives at another perspective on information characteristics -information related to actual intentions or contents. Our results demonstrate that information content has a significant effect on information diffusion. When the type of information is "Information Providing", information diffusion is fast. In the 'Advertisement' type, the scale of diffusion is higher and the duration is longer than for the 'Information providing' type. In other words, the patterns of information diffusion vary according to information content. For a given dataset of content created by a firm, Twitter information delivery to users occurs according to a wide variety of diffusion characteristics.

Our findings have important implications for business management. Our research provides useful guidelines in terms of understanding information content on Twitter. The knowledge that the 'Information providing' type typically associates with the speed of diffusion and the 'Advertisement' type associated with the scale and duration of diffusion provides business with helpful advice. It specifies not only how to quickly spread information but also how to make sure that users continue to repost tweets based on specific attributes of tweet contents. It shows that firms can spread information more quickly by providing the 'Information and advertisement' type rather than the 'Advertisement' type.

This study has performed a careful analysis of the impact of information contents and user characteristics on information diffusion. However, as with any empirical study, it has limitations. One issue arises from the tweets sample used and data collected because we choose a particular firm, olleh_Mobile. The impact of information contents for improving information diffusion are likely to differ among various firms. It is recommended that samples from a broad range of industries be used in future research. Thus, it is important to study how diffusion happens differently across specific industries.

Acknowledgement. This research was supported by the MSIP (Ministry of Science, ICT&-Future Planning), Korea, under the ITRC (Information Technology Research Center) support program (NIPA-2014-H0301-14-1044) supervised by the NIPA (National ICT Industry Promotion Agency).

References

Bajwa, D.S., Lewis, L.F., Pervan, G., Lai, V.S., Munkvold, B.E., Schwabe, G.: Factors in the global assimilation of collaborative information technologies: an exploratory investigation in five regions. J. Manag. Inf. Syst. **25**(1), 131–165 (2008)

Barnes, S.J., BöHringer, M.: Modeling use continuance behavior in microblogging services: the case of twitter. J. Comput. Inf. Syst. **51**(1), 1–10 (2011)

Berinato, S.: Six ways to find value in twitter's noise. Harvard Bus. Rev. **88**(6), 34–35 (2010)

Boettger, R.K., Palmer, L.A.: Quantitative content analysis: its use in technical communication. IEEE Trans. Prof. Commun. **53**(4), 346–357 (2010)

Brancheau, J.C., Wetherbe, J.C.: The adoption of spreadsheet software: testing innovation diffusion theory in the context of end-user computing. Inf. Syst. Res. **1**(2), 115–143 (1990)

Cha, M., Haddadi, H., Benevenuto, F., Gummadi, P.K.: Measuring user influence in twitter: The million follower fallacy. In: Association for the Advancement of Artificial Intelligence (2010)

Chatman, E.A.: Diffusion theory: a review and test of a conceptual model in information diffusion. J. Am. Soc. Inf. Sci. **37**(6), 377–386 (1986)

Cheung, C., M.K, Lee, M.K.O., Rabjohn, N.: The impact of electronic word-of-mouth. The adoption of online opinions in online customer communities. Int. Res. **18**(3), 229-247 (2008)

Fichman, R.G.: Information technology diffusion: a review of empirical research. In: Proceedings of the 13th International Conference on Information Systems (1992)

Fischer, E., Reuber, A.R.: Social interaction via new social media: (how) can interactions on twitter affect effectual thinking and behavior? J. Bus. Ventur. **26**(1), 1–18 (2011)

Fullwood, C., Sheehan, N., Nicholls, W.: Blog function revisited: a content analysis of myspace blogs. CyberPsychol. Behav. **12**(6), 685–689 (2009)

Greer, C.F., Ferguson, D.A.: Using twitter for promotion and branding: a content analysis of local television twitter sites. J. Broadcast. Electron. Media. **55**(2), 198–214 (2011)

Ha, L., James, E.L.: Interactivity reexamined: a baseline analysis of early business web sites. J. Broadcast. Electron. Media. **42**, 457–474 (1998)

Herring, S.C., Scheidt, L.A., Kouper, I., Wright, E.: A Longitudinal Content Analysis of Weblogs: 2003-2004. Routledge, London (2004)

Jansen, B.J., Zhang, M., Sobel, K., Chowdury, A.: twitter power: tweets as electronic word of mouth. J. Am. Soc. Inform. Sci. Technol. **60**(11), 2169–2188 (2009)

Java, A., Song, T.F., Tseng, B.: Why we twitter: understanding microblogging usage and communities. In: Proceedings of the Ninth WEBKDD and First SNA-KDD Workshop on Web Mining and Social Network Analysis, pp. 56–65 (2007)

Kaplan, A.M., Haenlein, M.: Users of the world, unite! the challenges and opportunities of social media. Bus. Horiz. **53**(1), 59–68 (2010)

Kim, H., Son, I., Lee, D.: The viral effect of online social network on new products promotion: investigating information diffusion on twitter. J. Intell. Inf. Syst. **18**(2) (2012)

Kruskal, W.H., Wallis, W.A.: Use of ranks in one-criterion variance analysis. J. Am. Stat. Assoc. **47**(260), 583–621 (1957)

Li, J., Rao, H.R.: Twitter as a rapido response news service: an exploration in the context of the 2008 china earthquake. Electron. J. Inf. Syst. Dev. Countries. **42**(4), 1–22 (2010)

Lin, J.-S., Pena, J.: Are you following me? a content analysis of tv networks' brand communication on twitter' the purpose of using twitter. J. Interact. Advertising. **12**(1), 17–29 (2011)

Miaskiewicz, T., Monarchi, D.E.: A review of the literature on the empathy construct using cluster analysis. Commun. AIS **22**, pp. 117–142 (2008)

Morris, R.: Computerized content analysis in management research: a demonstration of advantages and limitations. J. Manag. **20**(4), 903–931 (1994)

Naaman, M., Boase, J., Lai, C.-H.: Is it really about me? Message content in social awareness streams. In: CSCW (2010)

Papacharissi, Z.: The blogger revolution? audiences as media producers. In: The Annual Conference of the International Communication Association, New Orleans (2004)

Punj, G., Stewart, D.W.: Cluster analysis in marketing research: review and suggestions for application. J. Mark. Res. **20**, 134–148 (1983)

Rogers, E.M.: The Diffusion of Innovations. Free Press, New York (1983)

Rogers, E.M.: Diffusion of Innovations. Free Press, New York (2003)

Rogers, E.M., Shoemaker, F.F.: New York: Free Press (1971)

Savage, N.: Twitter as medium and message. Commun. ACM **54**(3), 18–20 (2011)

Segars, A.H., Grover, V.: Profiles of strategic information systems planning. Inf. Syst. Res. **10** (3), 199 (1999)

Simmons, L.L., Conlon, S., Mukhopadhyay, S., Yang, J.: A computer aided content analysis of online reviews. J. Comput. Inf. Syst. **52**, 43–55 (2011)

Sledgianowski, D., Kulviwat, S.: Using social network sites: the effects of playfulness, critical mass and trust in a hedonic context. J. Comput. Inf. Syst. **49**(4), 74–83 (2009)

Smith, B.G.: Socially distributing public relations: twitter, haiti, and interactivity in social media. Pub. Relat. Rev. **36**(4), 329–335 (2010)

Thelwall, M., Buckley, K., Paltoglou, G.: Sentiment in twitter events. J. Am. Soc. Inf. Sci. Technol. **62**(2), 406–418 (2011)

Yang, J., Counts, S.: Predicting the speed, scale, and range of information diffusion in twitter. In: 4th International AAAI Conference on Weblogs and Social Media (ICWSM) (2010)

Zhang, W., Watts, S.A.: Capitalizing on content: information adoption in two online communities. J. Assoc. Inf. Syst. **9**(2), 72–93 (2008)

Zhao, D., Rosson, M.B.: How and why people twitter: the role that micoblogging plays in informal communication at work. In: Proceedings of the ACM 2009 International Conference on Supporting Group Work, Sanibel Island, FL, pp. 243–252 (2009)

Multi-modal Similarity Retrieval
with a Shared Distributed Data Store

David Novak$^{(\boxtimes)}$

Masaryk University, Brno, Czech Republic
david.novak@fi.muni.cz

Abstract. We propose a generic system architecture for large-scale similarity search in various types of digital data. The architecture combines contemporary highly-scalable distributed data stores with recent efficient similarity indexes and also with other types of search indexes. The system is designed to provide several types of queries – distance-based similarity queries, term-based queries, attribute queries, and advanced queries combining several search aspects (modalities). The first part of this work is devoted to the generic architecture and to description of a similarity index PPP-Codes that is suitable for our system. In the second part, we describe a specific instance of this architecture that manages a 106 million image collection providing content-based visual search, keyword search, attribute-based access, and their combinations.

Keywords: Similarity search · Multi-modal search · Big Data · Scalability

1 Introduction and Motivation

The nature and volume of data has changed dramatically in recent years, which makes permanent pressure on data management and retrieval methods. The phenomenon of Big Data requires highly scalable techniques to provide efficient access to a large variety of data types that are often semi-structured or unstructured. For these kinds of data, it is often essential that the access methods are based on mutual similarity of the data objects because it corresponds to the human perception of the data or because exact matching would be too restrictive (various multimedia, biomedical or sensor data, etc.).

Should an access method be widely applicable, it must adopt a broad model of data; we primarily focus on generic *distance-based similarity* modeled by a data domain accompanied by a distance function to assess dissimilarity between each pair of objects from that domain [21]. The research field that adopts this data model covers many nontrivial tasks that have been subject of research for many years leading to a number of interesting results. Objective of this work is to build on these results to design a universal distributed data management and retrieval system that should (1) be highly scalable in terms of data volume and query throughput, (2) provide similarity data access based on generic data models, and (3) that should also allow traditional attribute- or key-based access and efficient combination of the conventional and similarity search.

© Institute for Computer Sciences, Social Informatics and Telecommunications Engineering 2015
J. Jung et al. (Eds.): INFOSCALE 2014, LNICST 139, pp. 28–37, 2015.
DOI: 10.1007/978-3-319-16868-5_3

A number of distributed structures for generic similarity search were proposed during the last decade [5,13,14,17]. The general basis of these techniques is to partition and organize the data collection according to similarity relationships of the data items; given a query point, the index can access selectively the query-relevant data partitions and refine them. In practice, data objects often have multiple fields (attributes, features, descriptors, annotations) and thus different access patterns (and their combinations) are very important (multi-modal search). A general disadvantage of partitioning and distributing data according to one similarity-based modality is an inefficient access by other modalities – via object ID, attributes, or other types of similarity; the primary similarity-based partitioning is typically dynamic which complicates building efficient indexes on other modalities. An available solution is to keep the data replicated and organized separately for each modality but this naturally causes consistency and efficiency issues and combined multi-aspect search is relatively difficult.

The fundamental feature of the generic architecture proposed in this paper (Sect. 2) is that the data objects are stored only once in a central distributed key-value store and they are directly accessible by object ID. Various (similarity) indexes are built "around" this central store and they process incoming queries, typically generating a *candidate set* of IDs that is then post-processed in the central store in a distributed way. The post processing can be either simple refinement of the candidate set, re-ranking with the aid of a different modality, or, for instance, filtering by given attributes. We assume that the search indexes manage only metadata and are capable of managing large collections; recently, a few similarity indexes were proposed that are well suited for our needs because they generate a very small set of candidate objects identified by their IDs [1,19].

This architecture is generic and very flexible allowing many access patterns and their combinations; we mention a few general options and describe in detail an instance of this architecture that enables large-scale multi-aspect image retrieval (Sect. 3). Scalability of the system is mainly assured by the central distributed store, which can be any mature key-value store which provides efficient data distribution, replication and dynamic adaptation of HW resources. Also, this store can manage data from different collections, each having own search indexes; this approach results in an effective resource utilization and is suitable for running the application as a service.

2   Similarity Retrieval on Big Data

In this section, we better specify the problem and the data model, then we describe the generic distributed architecture for Big Data similarity retrieval, and finally we sketch the principles of the similarity index PPP-Codes.

2.1   Distance-Based Similarity Search

The key feature of the proposed system is generic similarity search. We assume data model based on mutual object distances, specifically, $\mathcal{D}$ is a *domain of data* and δ is a total *distance* (dissimilarity) function $\delta : \mathcal{D} \times \mathcal{D} \longrightarrow \mathbb{R}_0^+$; we further assume that this domain and distance satisfy postulates of *identity*, *symmetry*, and many specific search techniques assume also *triangle inequality* [21]. A similarity index $I_\mathcal{X}$ organizes a subset of the data domain $\mathcal{X} \subseteq \mathcal{D}$ so that it can be searched efficiently using the *Query-by-example* paradigm; we mainly focus on the *nearest neighbors query* k-NN(q), which returns k objects from $\mathcal{X}$ with the smallest distances to given $q \in \mathcal{D}$: $\delta(q,x)$, $x \in \mathcal{X}$ (ties broken arbitrarily).

The field of distance-based similarity search has been studied for almost two decades now [9,10,21]. The problem in its generality is very difficult and for large data collections it is necessary to assume *approximate search*, which means that the search result may be an approximation of the precise k-NN answer defined above. A number of authors have turned their attention in this direction [20]. A typical general behavior of an approximate distance-based index $I_\mathcal{X}$ is that, given a query k-NN(q), $I_\mathcal{X}$ determines a set of candidate objects $C_\mathcal{X} \subseteq \mathcal{X}$ and this set is refined by explicit evaluation of $\delta(q,c)$, $c \in C_\mathcal{X}$. Typically, accessing and processing of this candidate set is hidden "inside" the index, e.g. [12,16].

Recently, there emerged a few indexes that can determine a relatively very small set of candidate objects identified by their IDs and these objects are to be retrieved from an external storage and checked one by one [1,19]; see Fig. 1 for a schema of this process. In this work, we exploit this type of indexes, specifically, we use the PPP-Index [19] briefly described in Sect. 2.4.

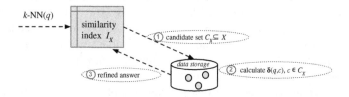

Fig. 1. Schema of basic similarity search using index $I_\mathcal{X}$.

2.2   Generic Architecture for Big Data Similarity Retrieval

A similarity index as described in the previous section is an important building block but a fully-fledged system for Big Data similarity management requires more than that. First, the real data are typically not simple objects from one similarity domain $(\mathcal{D}, \delta)$ but are rather compound. We model this in a standard way by assuming that each object x is composed of several *fields* (descriptors, attributes), each *field* being from data domain $\mathcal{D}_{field}$; we use notation $x.field \in \mathcal{D}_{field}$. Every object has a unique identifier $x.$ID and we can represent the whole object in JSON format as in the following example:

```
x1 = {"ID": "image_1",
       "keywords": "summer, beach, ocean, sun, sand",
       "color_histogram_descriptor": [25, 36, 0, 127, 69,... ],
       "shape_descriptor": [0.35, 1.24, 0.1, 0.45, 2.0,... ],
       "author": "David Novak",
       "date": 20140327 }
```

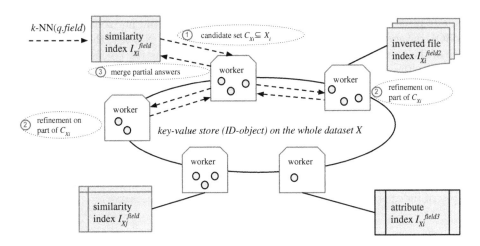

Fig. 2. Schema of Generic Architecture for Big Data similarity retrieval.

In general, different objects can have different fields. We assume that if domain $\mathcal{D}_{field}$ is to be explored via similarity, it has a corresponding distance function δ_{field}; other fields may be used for a different type of data access (attributed-based, keyword-based) or can be used for filtering.

Further, the overall indexed set $\mathcal{X}$ can be partitioned into several collections $\mathcal{X} = \mathcal{X}_1 \cup \mathcal{X}_2 \cup \cdots \cup \mathcal{X}_s$. Then, similarity index $I_{\mathcal{X}_i}^{field}$ can process query k-NN($q.field$), $q.field \in \mathcal{D}_{field}$ that returns the k objects from $\mathcal{X}_i$ that are the most similar according to distance $\delta_{field}(q.field, x.field)$, $x \in \mathcal{X}_i$.

At this point, we can describe the proposed architecture – see Fig. 2 for the general schema. The core of the system is a (typically distributed) key-value store indexing the whole dataset $\mathcal{X}$ according to the object IDs. We assume usage of any structure based on the idea of Amazon Dynamo [11] such as Riak[1], project Voldemort[2], or Infinispan[3]. Various search indexes are connected to this core component, each built on a sub-collection $\mathcal{X}_i$ (or on several sub-collections); these indexes can be both similarity and other types (inverted files for keywords search, B$^+$-tree for attribute fields). In general, we assume that, given a query k-NN($q.field$), index $I_{\mathcal{X}_i}^{field}$ generates candidate set $C_{\mathcal{X}_i}$ composed of object IDs from $\mathcal{X}_i$ (step 1 in Fig. 2); this candidate set is processed in a distributed way using the key-value core – the query is sent to those nodes (workers) that store part of $C_{\mathcal{X}_i}$, the candidate set is processed there (step 2), and partial answers are returned and merged (step 3).

Some contemporary key-value or document stores provide custom (distributed) attribute or full-text indexes to speedup selective access to the data (e.g., Riak, MongoDB[4]); these features can incorporated in our architecture. We can

---

[1] http://basho.com/riak/.
[2] http://www.project-voldemort.com.
[3] http://www.jboss.org/infinispan/.
[4] http://www.mongodb.org.

see our proposal as a way to exploit the strengths of the horizontally-scalable NoSQL databases also for similarity data management. Namely, the distributed core of the system should provide balanced data sharding (by consistent hashing on object IDs [11]), optionally data replication (for fault tolerance or for higher query traffic), and dynamic adaptation of HW resources (adding new worker nodes if the data volume or query traffic grow). We assume that individual indexes can cope with large data collections and searching within the indexes can be speeded up by parallel processing or, potentially, it can be another distributed structure like M-Chord [18]; the demanding process of candidate refinement is parallelized by the distributed store. This all should lead to a very good scalability of the system both in terms of stored data and search query traffic. Specific types of indexes convenient for this task are mentioned below.

2.3 Search and Update Queries

The general system architecture was designed not only for processing standard k-NN($q.field$) similarity queries as mentioned above; let us describe how the system can support other variants of search and update queries.

ID-object query. All search queries that work on the *query-by-example* principle, like the k-NN($q.field$), require having the *example* at hand ($q.field$). In real systems, the query object q is often from within the dataset $\mathcal{X}$ and is thus specified only by $q.ID$; in this case, the core key-value store of our system can be directly used to retrieve object q and initiate the similarity search with $q.field$.

k-NN query with filtering. The system can directly process query k-NN($q.field$) where the answer objects must match some additional attribute filter. The filtering can be easily applied during the candidate set refinement because it is realized on the whole compound data objects stored in the central data store.

Fusion query. Individual object fields naturally provide different search *modalities* (aspects). For many data types, e.g. multimedia, the *multimodal* search seems to be necessary to achieve satisfactory results [2]; our system inherently allows so-called *late fusion* approach, where the candidate set is identified by one modality, let say by $q.field$, but the final ranking of the result can be realized using a combination of several modalities [2]. Another useful search mode is to process a query, display it to the user, and allow them to initiate re-ranking of the result by a different (combined) modality; this can be realized in our system efficiently in a distributed manner similarly as candidate set refinement.

Updates. Insert/delete operations must be realized on search indexes on corresponding sub-collection $\mathcal{X}_i$ and the compound object x is inserted/delete into/ from the central store according to $x.ID$. Any updates on the stored data (adding/ removal/modification of individual fields) are realized directly in the central store (the data is stored only once) and, if need be, the search index on the particular field is updated.

2.4 PPP-Codes Similarity Index

The key to efficiency of similarity search realized by the proposed system is the index that determines a candidate set of objects close to given query q. Recently, we have proposed a technique called PPP-Codes [19] that is well suited for this purpose. Let us briefly describe this technique; to simplify the notation, we use the problem formulation from Sect. 2.1 with a simple search domain $(\mathcal{D}, \delta)$.

The basic task of a distance-based search technique is to *partition* the indexed collection $\mathcal{X} \subseteq \mathcal{D}$ only with the aid of the black-box pair-wise distance $\delta : \mathcal{D} \times \mathcal{D} \longrightarrow \mathbb{R}$. Majority of the distance-based approaches use *pivots* – objects selected from $\mathcal{X}$ (or from $\mathcal{D}$) that form certain anchors for data collection partitioning and search space pruning [21]. The PPP-Codes use a static set of pivots and apply *recursive Voronoi partitioning* of the data space [16,19]; such partitioning is sketched in Fig. 3 (left) for four pivots. The thick solid lines depict borders between standard Voronoi cells (points $x \in \mathcal{D}$ for which pivot p_i is the closest one) and the dashed lines further partition each cell using the other pivots. This principle is used in several techniques [8,12,16] and it is usually formalized as *pivot permutations* (PPs) – each recursive Voronoi cell is identified by the *indexes of the closest pivots*, for instance, cell $C_{4,1}$ contains all points for which pivot p_4 is the closest one and p_1 the second closest. These vectors of indexes are *pivot permutation prefixes* (PPPs) and are the base of the PPP-Codes technique.

Given such partitioning, another task is to identify cells relevant to given query $q \in \mathcal{D}$. This is done based on the query-pivot distances (depicted in Fig. 3, left); in complex data spaces, it is not easy to decide which cells are the closest ones from the query point and thus a relatively large number of objects $x \in \mathcal{X}$ must be accessed and refined by evaluation of distance $\delta(q, x)$. This level of complexity is caused by the fact that the data partitions typically span relatively large areas of the space and thus the candidate sets are either large or imprecise. The key idea of the PPP-Codes is to use several independent partitionings of the data space; given a query, each partitioning generates a ranked candidate set and the PPP-Codes index has a way to effectively and efficiently aggregate

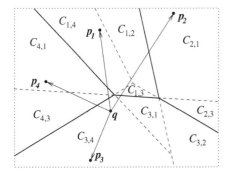
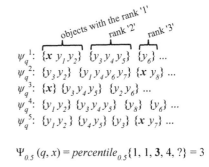

Fig. 3. Left: Example of second level Voronoi Partitioning using four pivots. Right: Rank aggregation by percentile of candidate ranks of individual objects.

these rankings. This aggregation is exemplified in Fig. 3 (right); each of five space partitionings generates a candidate ranking of indexed objects ψ_q^j, $j \in \{1, \ldots, 5\}$ and the final aggregated rank of each object is a certain *percentile* of its candidate ranks. In Fig. 3 (right), the median (0.5-percentile) of the five ranks of object x is 3 and thus the final rank $\Psi_{0.5}(q, x) = 3$.

The PPP-Codes propose an indexing structure and an algorithm to efficiently compute individual candidate ranks and their aggregation [19]. The aggregation is able to significantly shrink the candidate set while preserving its accuracy; the exact numbers are data dependent, but, for instance, to achieve 90 % recall on 10-NN queries, an average candidate set size is about 0.01 % of the dataset (measured on three diverse datasets) [19]. This result is about two orders of magnitude smaller than results from a single pivot space partitioning [12,16,19].

3   Specific System: Large-Scale Image Management

Let us now instantiate the general system architecture and describe a specific application system that can be built with this generic idea. The system should efficiently manage large collections of digital images and provide various types of access to this data with a primary focus on content-based similarity search.

The CoPhIR dataset [3,7] is a benchmark in large-scale visual image retrieval. It contains rich metadata for 106 million images downloaded from Flickr[5], especially it has five content descriptors suitable for global visual similarity comparison of the images. An image record can be represented as follows:

```
{ "ID": "002561195",
  "title": "My wife & daughter on Gold Coast beach",
  "tags": "summer, beach, ocean, sun, sand, Australia",
  "mpeg7_scalable_color": [25, 36, 0, 127, 69, ...],
  "mpeg7_color_layout": [[25, 41, 53, 20, 12, 4], [32, ...]],
  "mpeg7_color_structure": [0, 0, 1, 255, 32, 4, 0, ...],
  "mpeg7_edge_histogram": [5, 1, 2, 3, 7, 7, 3, 6, ...],
  "mpeg7_homogeneous_texture": [[232], [201], [198, 180,...]],
  "GPS_coordinates": [45.50382, -73.59921],
  "flickr_user": "david_novak" }
```

Individual fields are used for different data access as described below. But first, let us describe the overall architecture of the image retrieval system. The core of the system is an distributed ID-object store implemented using Infinispan[6], which is a Java-based project that provides API for executing operations on those nodes that manage certain subsets of keys, which is exactly what we need for post-processing of the candidate sets from the search indexes (see Sect. 2.2). The schema of the system is sketched in Fig. 4.

Each worker node of the distributed structure is composed of two layers: One participates in the core ID-object store and the other contains search index(es). In the figure, the specific indexes are magnified and they are described below.

---

[5] http://www.flickr.com.
[6] http://www.jboss.org/infinispan/.

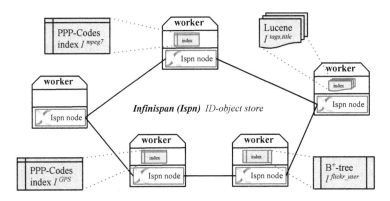

Fig. 4. Schema of distributed system for large-scale image retrieval on CoPhIR.

Visual Similarity Index. The CoPhIR objects contain fields with five MPEG-7 global visual descriptors [15] exploited for content-based visual similarity search in our system; the first three descriptors capture the color characteristics of the image and the other two are texture descriptors. There is a similarity measure recommended for each of the descriptor [3,15] and we build a *single search index* on a combination of these descriptors; this combination is realized as a *weighted sum* of distances between corresponding descriptors from query and data objects [3,4]. We use the PPP-Codes index (Sect. 2.4) to build a similarity search index on such combination – it is denoted as I^{mpeg7} in Fig. 4. As mentioned in Sect. 2.3, the index generates a candidate set of image IDs and, during its refinement, it can be further filtered and/or re-ranked by a combination with other search modality (e.g. annotations).

Annotation Search. The CoPhIR dataset contains several text-annotation fields (*title, tags, comments*); we have built a Lucene[7] index on the *titles* and *tags* (the *comments* are a bit messy and provided only for 12 % of the images [7]). This Lucene index $I^{tags,title}$ is used for (1) standard annotation-based search on the images and for (2) search that combines text and visual search in the following way: given a text search result, the user can issue a query that *re-ranks* this result with respect to visual similarity from given selected example image. This re-ranking is done in a distributed manner on the Infinispan nodes.

GPS Location Search. About 8 % of the CoPhIR images contain information about their GPS location [7]. We have built the PPP-Codes index I^{GPS} on the geographic distance for this subset of images. Again, the GPS location information can be also used during processing of candidate sets from other modalities.

Flickr Users. In order to demonstrate the universality of our approach, we have built also a standard B$^+$-tree on the `flickr_user` attribute; the leaf nodes of the tree contain object IDs that can be further processed by the Infinispan store.

---

[7] http://lucene.apache.org/.

Practical Experience

The whole system is implemented using Java with the aid of implementation framework for similarity search MESSIF [6]. The system is very flexible in terms of hardware infrastructure it can run on, ranging from a simulation on a single node to a large cluster for massive query load. Efficiency of the similarity search naturally depends on the HW infrastructure and on the precision of the approximate search which affects the candidate set size; the level of approximation in PPP-Codes can be tuned with respect to actual load of the system.

Detailed evaluation of the search performance is out of scope of this work but let us mention a single setting: the system was running on a single server with 8-core Intel Xeon @ 2.0 GHz with 12 GB of main memory and SATA SSD disk (measured transfer rate up to 400 MB/s with random accesses); the data occupied over 100 GB. Focusing on the MPEG7 visual search, the PPP-Codes index I^{mpeg7} occupied 4.6 GB having five pivot spaces each with 512 pivots [19]; to achieve 85 % recall on 10-NN search, candidate set of 5000 objects (out of 106 million) must be refined. With this settings, average response times are about 750 ms and the system can resolve about three queries per second.

4 Conclusions

An efficient generic similarity search on the big scale is one of long-term goals in the area of data management since it would be very beneficial for many information retrieval tasks. We have described a flexible architecture that can combine latest similarity search techniques with contemporary highly scalable data stores. The core of the system is a distributed key-value store that organizes objects from one or more data collections based on object IDs. To this core, various search indexes can be connected with a focus on similarity search. Given a query, the index produces a candidate set of object IDs, which is refined in a distributed manner by the core data store. The data objects can have various fields of different types and also the search queries can be variable, especially, (1) similarity *queries by example* on a single search modality, (2) the basic similarity search enriched by filtering or post-ranking with the aid of other modality, (3) results of one search query can be re-ranked by completely different criteria.

We have built a specific system that manages the CoPhIR collection of 106 million images [7]. The system uses the Infinispan as the core distributed key-value store and our PPP-Codes index [19] for visual similarity search and for geographic distance search; further, we use Lucene for search on annotations and B$^+$-tree on attribute data. The similarity search is very efficient, achieving response times about 750 ms and throughput about three queries per second on a single standard machine and scaling up with stronger HW infrastructure.

Acknowledgments. This work was supported by Czech Research Foundation project P103/12/G084.

References

1. Amato, G., Gennaro, C., Savino, P.: MI-File: using inverted files for scalable approximate similarity search. In: Multimedia Tools and Applications, pp. 1–30 (2012)
2. Atrey, P.K., Hossain, M.A., El Saddik, A., Kankanhalli, M.S.: Multimodal fusion for multimedia analysis: a survey. Multimedia Syst. **16**, 345–379 (2010)
3. Batko, M., Falchi, F., Lucchese, C., Novak, D., Perego, R., Rabitti, F., Sedmidubsky, J., Zezula, P.: Building a web-scale image similarity search system. Multimed. Tools Appl. **47**(3), 599–629 (2010)
4. Batko, M., Kohoutkova, P., Novak, D.: CoPhIR image collection under the microscope. In: Proceedings of SISAP 2009, pp. 47–54. IEEE (2009)
5. Batko, M., Novak, D., Falchi, F., Zezula, P.: On scalability of the similarity search in the world of peers. In: Proceedings of InfoScale 2006, pp. 1–12. ACM Press, New York, USA (2006)
6. Batko, M., Novak, D., Zezula, P.: MESSIF: metric similarity search implementation framework. In: Thanos, C., Borri, F., Candela, L. (eds.) Digital Libraries: Research and Development. LNCS, vol. 4877, pp. 1–10. Springer, Heidelberg (2007)
7. Bolettieri, P., Esuli, A., Falchi, F., Lucchese, C., Perego, R., Piccioli, T., Rabitti, F.: Cophir: a test collection for content-based image retrieval. CoRR 0905.4 (2009)
8. Chávez, E., Figueroa, K., Navarro, G.: Effective proximity retrieval by ordering permutations. IEEE Trans. Pattern Anal. Mach. Intell. **30**(9), 1647–1658 (2008)
9. Chávez, E., Navarro, G., Baeza-Yates, R., Marroquín, J.L.: Searching in metric spaces. ACM Comput. Surv. **33**(3), 273–321 (2001)
10. Ciaccia, P., Patella, M., Zezula, P.: M-Tree: an efficient access method for similarity search in metric spaces. In: Proceedings of VLDB 1997, vol. 25, pp. 426–435 (1997)
11. DeCandia, G., Hastorun, D., Jampani, M., Kakulapati, G., Lakshman, A., Pilchin, A., Sivasubramanian, S., Vosshall, P., Vogels, W.: Dynamo: amazons highly available key-value store. ACM SIGOPS Operating Syst. Rev. **41**(6), 205–220 (2007)
12. Esuli, A.: Use of permutation prefixes for efficient and scalable approximate similarity search. Inf. Process. Manage. **48**(5), 889–902 (2012)
13. Gil-Costa, V., Marin, M.: Approximate distributed metric-space search. In: Proceedings of LSDS-IR 2011, pp. 15–20. ACM Press, New York, USA (2011)
14. Malkov, Y., Ponomarenko, A., Logvinov, A., Krylov, V.: Scalable distributed algorithm for approximate nearest neighbor search problem in high dimensional general metric spaces. In: Navarro, G., Pestov, V. (eds.) SISAP 2012. LNCS, vol. 7404, pp. 132–147. Springer, Heidelberg (2012)
15. MPEG-7: Multimedia content description interfaces. Part 3: Visual. ISO/IEC 15938–3:2002 (2002)
16. Novak, D., Batko, M., Zezula, P.: Metric index: an efficient and scalable solution for precise and approximate similarity search. Inf. Syst. **36**(4), 721–733 (2011)
17. Novak, D., Batko, M., Zezula, P.: Large-scale similarity data management with distributed Metric Index. Inf. Process. Manage. **48**(5), 855–872 (2012)
18. Novak, D., Zezula, P.: M-Chord: a scalable distributed similarity search structure. In: Proceedings of InfoScale 2006, pp. 1–10. ACM Press, NY, USA (2006)
19. Novak, D., Zezula, P.: Rank aggregation of candidate sets for efficient similarity search. In: Decker, H., Lhotská, L., Link, S., Spies, M., Wagner, R.R. (eds.) DEXA 2014, Part II. LNCS, vol. 8645, pp. 42–58. Springer, Heidelberg (2014)
20. Patella, M., Ciaccia, P.: Approximate similarity search: a multi-faceted problem. J. Discret. Algorithms **7**(1), 36–48 (2009)
21. Zezula, P., Amato, G., Dohnal, V., Batko, M.: Similarity Search the Metric Space Approach. Advances in Database Systems, vol. 32. Springer, Heidelberg (2006)

An Efficient Approach for Complex Data Summarization Using Multiview Clustering

Mohiuddin Ahmed[(✉)], Abdun Naser Mahmood, and Michael J. Maher

School of Engineering and Information Technology,
UNSW Canberra, Canberra, ACT 2600, Australia
Mohiuddin.Ahmed@student.unsw.edu.au, {A.Mahmood,M.Maher}@unsw.edu.au

Abstract. There is significant interest in the data mining and network management communities to efficiently analyse huge amount of network traffic, given the amount of network traffic generated even in small networks. Summarization is a primary data mining task for generating a concise yet informative summary of the given data and it is a research challenge to create summary from network traffic data. Existing summarization techniques are based on clustering and frequent itemset mining which lacks the ability to create summary for further data mining tasks such as anomaly detection. Additionally, for complex and high dimensional network traffic dataset, there is often no single clustering solution that explains the structure of the given data. In this paper, we investigate the use of multiview clustering to create meaningful summary from network traffic data in an efficient manner. We develop a mathematically sound approach to select the summary size using a sampling technique. The main contribution of this paper is to propose a summarization technique for use in anomaly detection. Additionally, we also propose a new metric to evaluate summary based on the presence of normal and anomalous data instances. We validate our proposed approach using the benchmark network traffic dataset.

Keywords: Scalable data mining · Network traffic summarization · Multiview clustering

1 Introduction

Summarization is considered as a key knowledge discovery approach that produces a concise, yet informative version of the original dataset [3]. Clustering, which groups together similar data instances, is often used for summarization [4–7]. Among the large pool of clustering algorithms [8], *k-means* [9] clustering has been widely used since it is easy to implement and understand. The resulting cluster centroids are considered the summary of the original data. However, *k-means* introduces several problems in terms of summarizing a dataset. First, the *k-means* algorithm generates a centroid calculating the mean of the data instances within a cluster, which may not be an actual member of the dataset.

© Institute for Computer Sciences, Social Informatics and Telecommunications Engineering 2015
J. Jung et al. (Eds.): INFOSCALE 2014, LNICST 139, pp. 38–47, 2015.
DOI: 10.1007/978-3-319-16868-5_4

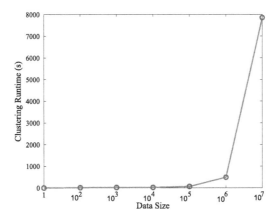

Fig. 1. Run time complexity

A summary produced using these centroids might be misleading. Another important problem for summarization using unsupervised techniques on unlabelled data is that the number of clusters is generally unknown. Importantly, traditional clustering techniques focus on producing only a single solution, even though multiple alternate clustering may exist. It is thus difficult for the user to validate whether the given solution is in fact appropriate, particularly if the dataset is large and high dimensional (such as network traffic), or if the user has limited knowledge about the clustering algorithm being used. In this case, it is highly desirable to provide another, alternative clustering solution, which is able to extract more information about the underlying pattern from different dimensions of the dataset.

Figure 1 shows the run time complexity of basic *k-means* [9] clustering algorithm on different sizes of data. It is clearly visible that, as data size increases the run time complexity also increases. As a result, knowledge discovery from large datasets becomes very inefficient. Consequently, summarization is a necessary step before performing data mining (such as anomaly detection from network traffic), which can expedite the process of knowledge discovery.

Rest of the paper contains the related works in Sect. 2, Multiview clustering and its relevance to complex data analysis is discussed in Sect. 3. We discuss our proposed approach in Sect. 4 and experimental results in Sect. 5. Section 6 concludes the paper.

2   Related Works

In this Section, we briefly review the existing clustering based summarization approaches. Although, there are different approaches of data summarization, the clustering based summarization approaches fall within the scope of this paper. Ha-Thuc et al. [5] proposed a quality-threshold data summarization method modifying the *k-means* algorithm. The number of cluster is determined using

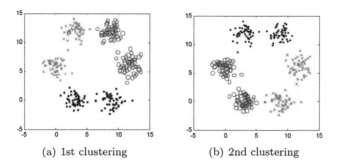

(a) 1st clustering   (b) 2nd clustering

Fig. 2. Two alternative clusterings of the same dataset, each with 3 clusters. Point shapes show cluster membership, adapted from [1].

the characteristics of dataset and a threshold. The algorithm partitions a dataset until the distortion or sum of squared error (SSE) is less than a given threshold. It starts by finding the cluster centroids as *k-means* but next steps are executed only if the SSE is above the given threshold and the existing cluster is split. New centroid is introduced which is closer to the larger cluster centroid. This process is repeated until all the clusters SSE exceeds the given threshold as input. They did not explain the method to choose the threshold and how the characteristics of datasets are analysed. Patrick et al. [6] proposed a distributed clustering framework, where the dataset is partitioned between several sites and output is mixture of gaussian models. Each distributed dataset is summarized using *k-means* algorithm and sent to a central site for global clustering. Prodip et al. [7] proposed an approach for clustering large datasets by randomly dividing the original data into disjoint subsets. The *k-means* algorithm is applied to summarize the dataset as well as to form ensemble using the centroids. Wagstaff et al. [4] presented a semi-supervised summarization approach for hyperspectral images. Hyperspectral images produce very large image in which each pixel is recorded at hundreds or thousands of different wavelengths. The ability to automatically generate summaries of these dataset enables important applications such as quickly browsing through a large image repository. However, this technique uses pre-specified knowledge to seed the initial centre for clustering which is not directly applicable in different domains.

3   Multiview Clustering

Exploratory data analysis aims to identify and generate multiple views of the structure within a dataset. Conventional clustering techniques [8], however, are designed to only provide a single grouping or clustering of a dataset. Data clustering is challenging, because there is no universal definition of it. Labelled data is generally not available that may help in the understanding of the underlying structure of the data, moreover, there is no unique similarity measure for differentiating clusters. Consequently, it is evident that there is no single clustering solution that explains the structure of a given dataset, especially if it is large (such as network traffic) and represented in a high dimensional space. This challenge has given rise to the recently emerging area of multiview clustering analysis [2], where goal is to explore different partitions, in order to describe different grouping aspects for a given dataset. For example, consider the data given in Fig. 2 and assume the number of clusters to be uncovered is 3. It is clear that both of the clustering solutions found in two Figs. 2a and 2b are equally valid and logical, since they fit the data well and have the same clustering quality. It would be difficult to justify keeping only the first clustering, while omitting the second. We can also identify similar examples in real life applications. For example, in network traffic analysis, one can cluster traffic instances by their basic attributes; or content attributes, both clustering solutions are equally important and each could be used to provide a different interpretation of the data. In this paper, we study the application of multiview clustering on summarization of large and high dimensional data.

3.1   Theoretical Background

Multiview clustering problem can be formulated using the information theoretic concepts. For example, if we are given a dataset X with N points, such as $X = (x_1, x_2, ..., x_N)$, the task is to find a set of alternative clustering solution, $C = (c_1, c_2...)$, where the clustering quality in terms of objective function will be high and simultaneously the clustering solutions will be highly dissimilar to one another i.e. mutual information $I(c_1; c_2)$ is close to zero and $c_1 \neq c_2$. Entropy is an important information theoretic measure to reflect uncertainty of information. For example, for a random variable R with probability distribution $p(r)$, the entropy can be defined using Eq. (1).

$$H(R) = - \int p(r) \, log \, p(r) \mathrm{d}r \qquad (1)$$

For a pair of random variable (R,S) their joint entropy can be estimated using Eq. (2).

$$H(R, S) = - \int \int p(r, s) \, log \, p(r, s) \mathrm{d}r \mathrm{d}s \qquad (2)$$

Now, mutual information can be defined as the relative entropy between the joint distribution $p(r,s)$ and the product of two marginal distributions $p(r)p(s)$ as given in Eq. (3).

$$I(R, S) = \int \int p(r, s) \, log \, \frac{p(r, s)}{p(r)p(s)} drds \qquad (3)$$

3.2   Network Traffic as Complex Data

Network traffic can be considered as complex data where the straightforward data mining applications may not be effective. Data comes from more than one process. Each entry in the dataset is usually not only the outcome of a single characteristic; but also the combination different process. The relationship among the attributes is not always significant. Moreover, network traffic dataset contains mixed attributes and thus the relationship among the attributes is quite insignificant.

4   Proposed Multiview Clustering Based Network Traffic Summary

In this Section, we describe our proposed method for network traffic summarization. At first we discuss about the necessity of sampling and the statistical approach to calculate the summary size. Then we explain our algorithm and the metric we propose for network traffic summarization.

4.1   Sampling Methods

The rationale behind integrating the sampling methods for summarization is based on the need to represent actual data instances in the summary unlike other existing methods discussed in Sect. 2 that may have average or some other representative of the data in the summary. Sampling is a popular choice for reduction of input data in data mining and machine learning techniques.

For the network traffic summarization purpose, systematic sampling is advantageous over the simple random sampling and stratified sampling because it involves choosing the data instances to be sampled at equal intervals. However, it can suffer from periodicity of the data but we address the issue by using clustering. We think of choosing the samples from the clusters produced from the original dataset. Since, the clustering process groups together the similar data instances, the systematic sampling scheme will encompass the total cluster and be able to represent the cluster well. Additionally, this technique results better when the sample size is known and we plan to calculate the sample size of the produced cluster using statistical formula (discussed in next Sect. 4.2).

4.2   Sample Size Calculation

Sample size determination is a very important issue because large sample size is a wastage of time and resource; on the other hand smaller sample may lead to wrong results [12]. In this scenario, sample mean and the original dataset mean is different and this difference is considered as an error. The margin of error E is the maximum difference between the sample mean and the original dataset mean. According to Walpole et al. [12] view point, this error E, can be defined using the following Eq. (4). Where, $z_{\alpha/2}$ is the critical value; σ is the dataset standard deviation and n is the sample size. After rearranging Eq. (4), the sample size (summary size) can be calculated (5)

$$E = z_{\alpha/2} * \frac{\sigma}{\sqrt{n}} \qquad (4)$$

$$n = \left[\frac{z_{\alpha/2} * \sigma}{E}\right]^2 \tag{5}$$

4.3 Multiview Clustering Based Network Traffic Summarization

In this Section, we describe our proposed algorithm for creating summary using the aforementioned data mining and statistical theories.

MCNTS (Multiview Clustering based Network Traffic Summarization)

Input: D, Dataset.
Output: S, the summary of D.
Method:
Begin
1.   *Multiview Clustering$(D) = C_1, C_2, ...C_k$*
2.   ***for*** each clustering solution C_i, $i = 1{:}k$
3.   Calculate the summary size (5)
4. $S_i = Representative\ Sample\ of\ C_i$
5.   ***end***
6. $S = Union\ i{=}1....k\ \{S_i\}$
End

In the MCNTS algorithm, our proposed framework for network traffic summarization is presented. At first, we apply *k-means* clustering on the network traffic dataset [13] which has four different attribute types. For multiview clustering, we apply *k-means* clustering on each of the attribute types of the dataset assuming that, the dataset contains only normal and attack traffic. So, the number of clusters in the dataset is considered as two. Next, from each of the clustering solution, we calculate the sample/summary size using the statistical theories discussed in previous Sect. 4.2. Once the summary size of the cluster is calculated, we take representative sample from the cluster having original data instances using systematic sampling. The representative sample has the minimum difference between the cluster centroid and mean of the selected sample. Finally, we merge all the representative samples from all the clustering solutions produced to create the final summary. Our proposed approach overcomes the problems with the existing summarization techniques where the sample size and the representation of original data in the summary are the main constraints. Additionally, the summary produced by our approach can be used as an input to anomaly detection techniques.

4.4 New Summarization Metric: Adaptability

$$\begin{aligned} Adaptability &= a1/A + n1/N + a2/A + n2/N + ... + as/A + ns/N \\ &= (a1 + a2 + ... + as)/A + (n1 + n2 + ... + ns)/N \end{aligned} \tag{6}$$

Our aim is to create summaries that can be useful for anomaly detection and such summary may contain two types of data instances, one belonging to normal behaviour and the other belonging to attacks. In addition to existing summarization metrics, such as conciseness, information loss, in this paper we propose a new metric *Adaptability*; that reflects the amount of normal and attack data instances present in the summary. Adaptability can be defined as follows (6), where s represent the number of individual summary elements S_i and a Summary $S = \sum_{i=1}^{s}(S_i)$. Here a is the number of anomalous data in summary and A is the number of anomalous data in the original dataset, n/N represents the proportion of normal data in summary with respect to original data. Consequently, higher values of adaptability index refer to a summary's suitability as an input to anomaly detection technique.

5   Experimental Analysis

For our experimental analysis, we used a variant of benchmark KDD cup 1999 dataset. NSL-KDD dataset [13] is a short form KDD cup 1999 which is derived from DARPA 1998 data from Licoln Laboratory at MIT. KDD 1999 is the most widely utilized dataset for the evaluation of the anomaly detection methods on network traffic. NSL-KDD is a dataset suggested to solve some of the inherent problems of the KDD 1999 dataset as mentioned in [11].

5.1   Summarization Metrics

The summarization metrics discussed here were recently proposed and used specifically for network traffic summarization (For more details, please see [10]). **Conciseness** defines how compact a summary is with respect to the original dataset. It is the ratio of input dataset size and the summarized set size or ratio of the number of elements in the both sets (original and summarized). **Information Loss** is a general metric used to describe the amount of information lost from the original dataset as a result of the summarization. Loss is defined as the sum of all the ratios of attributes not present by attributes represented in the summary. **Interestingness** is a new summarization metric, which focused on the objective measures of interestingness with applicability to summarization, emphasizing on diversity. **Intelligibility** is used to measure how much meaningful a summary is based on the attributes present on the summary.

5.2   Discussion on Experimental Results

Table 1 displays the clustering solutions over different views (on different attribute types). It is clearly visible that, the multiview clustering (*k-means* on different attribute types of the given dataset) produces different clustering results. Figure 3 displays the data distribution of multiview clustering solutions. For each of the attribute type of network traffic, the clustering solution reflects a different

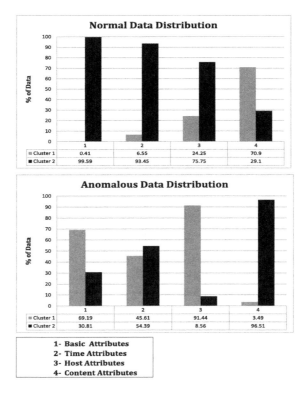

Fig. 3. Data distribution of multiview clustering solutions

data assignment. For example, the basic attributes clustering shows that, cluster 1 contains almost no normal traffic instances, whereas the content attributes clustering yields 70 % normal traffic instances in cluster 1. This scenario is also visible in case of the anomalous traffic instances, each of the attribute types yield different clustering solutions. Table 2 contains the clustering solution of regular *k-means* algorithm, which means clustering on the dataset considering all the attributes types together and that is why the Tables 1 and 2 is different.

Table 1. Multiview Clustering Results

Dataset	Basic	Host	Time	Content
Cluster-1	32.47 %	55.57 %	24.76 %	39.48 %
Cluster-2	67.53 %	44.43 %	75.24 %	60.52 %

In Table 3, we show the comparison with two other approaches. Regular clustering based approach performs basic *k-means* and creates two clusters because underlying data has normal and attack data instances. Once the clustering is

Table 2. Regular Clustering Results

Dataset	Number of instances
Cluster-1	35.06 %
Cluster-2	64.94 %

Table 3. Experimental results of the MCNTS algorithm

Technique	Conciseness	Information loss	Interestingness	Adaptability
MCNTS	47.62	0.90	0.04	4.35
Regular clustering	169.07	0.94	0.003	1.17
RANDOM	169.07	0.94	0.003	1.17

done, the summary size is calculated according to the methodology discussed in Sect. 4.2. We applied the sampling technique on regular clustering to compare with our proposed approach. Another approach is based on random scenario, which chooses summary data instances randomly to see whether our proposed technique is actually better than the existing ones. It is clearly stated in Table 3, that our approach has less information loss and significantly better adaptability than the other approaches. The proposed method also resulted in inferior conciseness, because of the merging of summaries from four different clustering solutions, whereas, the other approaches consider only one clustering solution. Since, all the attributes are present in the summary, intelligibility is equal in all case and interestingness also suggests that our approach is better. The regular clustering approach and random approach results are similar, because both the approaches were clustered in same way, however, the adaptability is expected to differ but due to the random selection, it reflects similar results.

6   Conclusion

In this paper, we addressed two major drawbacks of the existing clustering based summarization techniques. Summary size estimation and representing original data instances in the summary without losing any attribute are the key focus of this paper. Additionally, instead of using regular clustering algorithm for summarization, we use multiview clustering which is theoretically sound and more informative in nature for summarization. Our proposed algorithm uses sampling method pick original data instances to be added in the summary and statistical measure is used to calculate the sample size. Experimental analysis used the state-of-the-art evaluation metrics for summarization and we also proposed a new metric for summarization. In future, we will focus on real-time network traffic summarization.

References

1. Dang, X.H., Bailey, J.: Generation of alternative clusterings using the cami approach, In: SDM 2010, pp. 118–129 (2010)
2. Dang, X., Bailey, J.: A framework to uncover multiple alternative clusterings. Mach. Learn. **98**, 1–24 (2013)
3. Chandola, V., Kumar, V.: Summarization- compressing data into an informative representation. Knowl. Inf. Syst. **12**(3), 355–378 (2007)
4. Wagstaff, L., Shu, P., Mazzoni, D., Castano, R.: Semi-supervised data summarization: using spectral libraries to improve hyperspectral clustering. Interplanet. Netw. Prog. **42**, 1–14 (2005)
5. Ha-Thuc, V., Nguyen, D.-C., Srinivasan, P.: A quality-threshold data summarization algorithm. In: RIVF, pp. 240–246. IEEE (2008)
6. Wendel, P., Ghanem, M., Guo, Y.: Scalable clustering on the data grid. In: 5th IEEE International Symposium Cluster Computing and the Grid (CCGrid) (2005)
7. More, P., Hall, L.: Scalable clustering: a distributed approach. In: Proceedings of the IEEE International Conference on Fuzzy Systems 2004, vol. 1, pp. 143–148 (2004)
8. Jain, A.K., Murty, M.N., Flynn, P.J.: Data clustering: a review. ACM Comput. Surv. **31**(3), 264–323 (1999)
9. MacQueen, J.B.: Some methods for classification and analysis of multivariate observations. In: Cam, L.M.L., Neyman, J. (eds.) Proceedings of the fifth Berkeley Symposium on Mathematical Statistics and Probability, vol. 1, pp. 281–297. University of California Press (1967)
10. Hoplaros, D., Tari, Z., Khalil, I.: Data summarization for network traffic monitoring. J. Netw. Comput. Appl. **37**, 194–205 (2014)
11. John, M.: A critique of the 1998 and 1999 darpa intrusion detection system evaluations as performed by lincoln laboratory. ACM Trans. Inf. Syst. Secur. **3**(4), 262–294 (2000)
12. Walpole, M.: Fundamentals of Probability and Statistics. Prentice Hall, Englewood Cliffs (1980)
13. NSL-KDD Datasett. http://nsl.cs.unb.ca/NSL-KDD/. Accessed: 10 June 2014

Big Data Applications

A Novel Approach for Network Traffic Summarization

Mohiuddin Ahmed[(✉)], Abdun Naser Mahmood, and Michael J. Maher

School of Engineering and Information Technology,
UNSW Canberra, Canberra, ACT 2600, Australia
Mohiuddin.Ahmed@student.unsw.edu.au,
{A.Mahmood,M.Maher}@unsw.edu.au

Abstract. Network traffic analysis is a process to infer patterns in communication. Reliance on computer network and increasing connectivity of these networks makes it a challenging task for the network managers to understand the nature of the traffic that is carried in their network. However, it is an important data analysis task, given the amount of network traffic generated. Summarization is a key data mining concept, which is considered as a solution for creating concise yet accurate summary of network traffic. In this paper, we propose a new definition of summary for network traffic which outperforms the existing state-of-the-art summarization techniques. Our approach is based on clustering algorithm which reduces the information loss incurred by the existing techniques. By analysing the traffic summarization results using most up to date evaluation metrics, we demonstrate that our approach achieves better summaries than others on benchmark KDD cup 1999 dataset and also on real life network traffic including simulated attacks.

Keywords: Data summarization · Network traffic analysis · Clustering

1 Introduction

It is expected that each year internet traffic doubles. One of the open challenges for network and data professionals is analysing this huge amount of data in order to obtain knowledge. Computer network traffic is produced at a very fast rate and makes it a difficult task to monitor a network in real time [2]. Different application like *Email, FTP, HTTP, P2P* generate a huge amount of data, which cannot be analysed in real time [3]. One promising solution of this problem can be a summary, which can be analysed faster and contain similar knowledge. To address the problem mentioned above, network traffic analysis can be performed on summarized dataset and yet can achieve higher efficiency. So, summarization is a possible step to support real time monitoring and reduce time complexity in network traffic analysis.

Summarization is considered as a key knowledge discovery approach that produces a concise, yet informative version of the original dataset [4]. Clustering, which groups together similar data instances, is often used for semantic

© Institute for Computer Sciences, Social Informatics and Telecommunications Engineering 2015
J. Jung et al. (Eds.): INFOSCALE 2014, LNICST 139, pp. 51–60, 2015.
DOI: 10.1007/978-3-319-16868-5_5

summarization [8,9]. Among the large pool of clustering algorithms, *k-means* [6] clustering has been widely used for summarization since it is easy to implement and simple in nature. The resulting cluster centroids are considered as the summary of the original data. However, *k-means* introduces several problems in terms of summarizing a dataset. First, *k-means* algorithm generates a centroid by calculating the mean of the data instances within a cluster, which may not be an actual member of the dataset. Summary produced using these centroids might be misleading (explained in Sect. 2). Another important problem for summarization using unsupervised techniques on unlabelled data is that the number of clusters is generally unknown. According to frequent itemset based approach, a summary is created using feature-wise intersection of all transactions, in this scenario, all the network traffic instances [1,7]. However, this technique incurs significant information loss when traffic instances have fewer identical values. For normal traffic instances, it is very likely that, traffic attributes will have different values for different types of networking activities. In this scenario, creating summary based on feature-wise intersection will fail to create any meaningful summary.

Consequently, we need an efficient network traffic summarization technique so that, the summary more closely resembles the original network traffic. The fundamental requirement of a summary is that, every data item should be represented. Our contributions in this paper are as follows:

- We investigate the adaptation of clustering and feature-wise intersection approaches to create summary.
- We address the problem of summarizing network traffic containing categorical attributes.

The rest of this paper is organized as follows: Sect. 2 contains related works and the problem statement followed by Sect. 3 where the proposed approach is articulated. Section 4 includes the evaluation results along with brief description on the summarization metrics. We conclude our paper stating the future research directions in Sect. 5.

2   Related Works and Problem Statement

In this Section, we discuss how summary is created using clustering techniques and feature-wise intersection. Then, we formulate the problem statement.

2.1   *Centroid Based Summarization (CBD)*

According to this approach, '*Once the dataset is clustered, the cluster centroids are used to form the summary of the original dataset*'.

The basic *k-means* algorithm has been widely used for this type summarization [8,9]. However, we give an example here to demonstrate that, *k-means* algorithm fails to provide a meaningful and informative summary.

Table 1. Cluster of sample network traffic instances[a]

Pr	Svc	Fg	sB	dB	c	sC	sDHR	dHC	dHSC	dHSSPR	dHSDHR	dHSR
tcp	http	SF	224	1680	3	21	0.1	239	255	0	0.01	0
tcp	http	SF	232	1713	9	9	0	255	255	0	0	0
tcp	http	SF	222	1471	6	12	0.17	6	255	0.17	0.02	0
tcp	http	SF	204	569	9	9	0	9	255	0.11	0.03	0
tcp	http	SF	335	2415	9	29	0.07	9	255	0.11	0.04	0
tcp	http	SF	231	3105	7	8	0.25	104	255	0.01	0.02	0.01
tcp	http	SF	204	313	39	39	0	39	255	0.03	0.02	0
tcp	http	SF	202	1761	4	4	0	49	255	0.02	0.02	0
tcp	http	SF	224	1818	14	14	0	59	255	0.02	0.02	0
tcp	http	SF	207	626	24	24	0	69	255	0.01	0.02	0

[a]the attribute names are abridged for formatting.

Table 2. Summary of the dataset in Table 1 according to *Centroid based Summarization*

Pr	Svc	Fg	sB	dB	c	sC	sDHR	dHC	dHSC	dHSSPR	dHSDHR	dHSR
*	*	*	228.5	1547.1	12.4	16.9	0.059	83.8	255	0.048	0.02	0.001

We considered a sample of network traffic data from KDD cup 1999 dataset [11] as a cluster and when the centroid is calculated it is seen that the summary produced does not represent the original data well. Table 2 displays the summary of the dataset of Table 1. Here the summary is the mean or the average of the data instances which is not an actual member of the cluster and only two attributes out of thirteen are present from the original dataset which reflects significant information loss. Additionally, the categorical data cannot be handled properly using the centroid based technique i.e., the mean of *protocol* attribute values TCP, ICMP, UDP cannot be calculated like the *count* attribute values which are numerical. Also the number of clusters needs to be provided as an input of the algorithm and without having previous knowledge on the dataset, finding the optimal number of cluster is hardly possible.

2.2 Feature-Wise Intersection Based Summarization (FIBS)

Here we discuss about the feature-wise intersection used to define a summary [1,7]. The most recent paper on network traffic monitoring [1], which is an extension of [7], characterized a summary as a compressed version of a set of given network traffic. According to Chandola et al. [7], '*A summary S of a set of data instances T, is a set of individual summaries $S_1, S_2, ...S_l$ such that (i) each S_j represents a subset of T and (ii)every data instance $T_i \in T$ is represented by at least one $S_j \in S$. An individual summary will be treated as a feature-wise* *intersection of all the data instances covered by it, i.e., if S_j covers $T_1, T_2, ..., T_k$, then $S_j = \bigcap_{i=1}^{k} T_i$.'*

Table 3 displays the summary based on *FIBS* of the dataset in Table 1. Here it is visible that, only four out of thirteen attributes are present and might not help a network manager as the summary lacks meaningful information. However, Chandola et al. [7] stated that, clustering based approach can produce good summary because it can capture the frequent modes of behaviour. And performs poorly when the dataset contains outlying data instances. Interestingly, it is very likely that network traffic datasets will have outliers [10]. Also, the normal data instances might have different values (see Table 1) and in this case, feature-wise intersection resulted in a meaningless summary (Table 3).

Table 3. Summary of the dataset in Table 1 according to *Feature-wise Intersection based Summarization*

Pr	Svc	Fg	sB	dB	c	sC	sDHR	dHC	dHSC	dHSSPR	dHSDHR	dHSR
tcp	http	SF	*	*	*	*	*	*	255	*	*	*

Table 4. Summary of the dataset in Table 1 according to proposed summary definition

Pr	Svc	Fg	sB	dB	c	sC	sDHR	dHC	dHSC	dHSSPR	dHSDHR	dHSR
tcp	http	SF	223	1696.5	9	13	0	54	255	0.02	0.02	0

3   Proposed Approach

In this section, we discuss our proposed methodology. At first we define summary for network traffic and then explain our algorithm.

3.1   Definition of a Summary for Network Traffic

Proposed Summary Definition: *'A summary S of a set of network traffic instances N, is a set of individual summaries $S_1, S_2, ..., S_i, .., S_n$ such that (i) the individual summaries are the actual members of N and (ii) each S_i represents a group of similar data instances'*

As it was seen in Sect. 2, according to the *Centroid based (CBD)* technique, the produced summary rarely represent the original data, and in some extent, the summary produced using centroids of *k-means* algorithm might be incorrect. In the summary of network traffic instances, when actual instances are represented, it is more meaningful to the analysts. For example, Table 2 displays the summary of the network traffic instances of Table 1, here only dHSC (dstHostSrvCount) presents the actual member of the original data instances in the summary. Rest of the attributes would hardly make any sense to the analyst or there might be another intermediate step to infer this summary to a meaningful format which will cause more computational complexity, since the underlying assumption is that, the summary is meaningful when the actual data instances are present in the summary and each individual summary should represent a group of data instances. In this paper, we incorporate *k-medoid* algorithm to address the summarization problem. This algorithm is a variant of *k-means* but selects an actual member of the dataset to represent a group. For network traffic analysis, different types of clustering techniques [4] are used but the incorporation of *k-medoid* for summarization process has not been used in the literature for network traffic summarization to the best of our knowledge [5]. Table 4 displays the summary according to our proposed approach. Next, we describe our proposed algorithm for network traffic summarization.

Algorithm 1. *NTS(Network Traffic Summarization)* Algorithm

Input: D, Dataset

               k, size of the summary

Output: S', the final summary of D

Method:

1. *Begin*
2. *Preprocess(D) = D'*
3. *k-medoid(D',k) = $C_1, C_2, ..., C_k$*
4.   *for each cluster, i = 1:k*
5.   *S(i)* = centroid(C_i)
6.   *end*
7. *S = Union i=1....k {S(i)}*
8. *S' = Postprocess(S)*
9. *End*

Algorithm 2. *Preprocess(D)*

Input: D, Dataset

Output: D', Identical attributes of D

Method:

1. *Begin*
2. *[row,column] = size(D)*
3. *for all* column, find the attribute types
4.   *for i=1:column*
5.   *if* **iscategorical**(column(i)) = true
6.   *for i=1:row*
7.   *Convert the N unique categorical values to integer as 0 to N-1*
8.   *end*
9.   *end*
10. *Categorical attributes = column(i)*
11. *D' = D*
12. *End*

Algorithm 3. *Postprocess(S)*

Input: *S*, The Summary
Output: *S'*, The final summary of *D*
Method:
1. *Begin*
2. [row,column] = size(*S*)
3. *Categorical attributes = column(i)*
4. *Replace the integer values to categorical as in Preprocess Step*
5. *Final Summary = S'*
6. *End*

3.2   NTS(Network Traffic Summarization) Algorithm

The summary definition proposed in the previous Sect. 3.1 cannot handle categorical data. Here in this Section, we propose a summarization technique which can handle mixed data types, as shown in *Algorithm* 1. The Network Traffic Summarization (NTS) algorithm takes the dataset and the size of the expected summary as input parameters. The network manager/analyst decides the size of the expected summary based on the network; however, in future we will investigate to find out the summary automatically without any user specified input of summary size. The algorithm starts by pre-processing the input dataset. The pre-processing method is given in *Algorithm* 2. Pre-processing the data is necessary when data consists of different attribute types, network traffic instances consist of different data types, for example KDD cup 1999 has three types of data, e.g. the categorical values such as protocol (*TCP,UDP,ICMP*) are mapped to integer values between *0 and N-1*, where *N* is the number of unique categorical values, in this case $N = 3$ and mapped as *TCP = 0, UDP = 1, ICMP = 2*. The mapping of categorical data to integer has also been used in learning classifier systems and widely accepted to reduce the complexity of computation [13]. Once the pre-processing is done, *k-medoid* clustering is applied with the given input of expected summary size as the number of clusters to be formed. Then, the cluster centroids are collectively called a summary. Next, the produced summary needs to be post processed, since we changed the categorical attributes to integer values. In the post processing step, we replace the integer values we changed earlier in the pre-processing step with the corresponding categorical values and thus the final summary is produced. Next, we discuss the experimental analysis in Sect. 4.

4   Evaluation Results

In this section, we briefly describe few summarization metrics proposed in a recent paper [1]. Then we validate our proposed approach with benchmark KDD Cup 1999 dataset [11], which has been widely used in existing approaches [12]. We also used a real life network traffic dataset which includes simulated attacks [13]. The dataset contains fully labelled TCP data including attacks identified using snort rule base and available from [14]. We compare our proposed summarization technique with the feature-wise intersection based summarization technique proposed in [1,7]. We conducted our experiments on a MAC OS Mavericks with core i7 processor and 8 GB DDR3 RAM.

4.1   Summarization Metrics

The summarization metrics discussed here have been recently proposed and used specifically for network traffic summarization (For more details, please see [1]). **Conciseness** defines how compact a summary is with respect to the original dataset. It is the ratio of summarized set size and the input dataset size or ratio of the number of elements in the both sets (original and summarized). **Information Loss** is a general metric used to describe the amount of information lost from the original dataset as a result of the summarization. Loss is defined as the sum of the proportion of attribute values not represented in the summary. **Interestingness** emphasizes on diversity. **Intelligibility** is used to measure how meaningful a summary is based on the attributes present in the summary.

4.2   Experimental Results

Summarization size is considered as a constraint in summarization algorithms. Summary size, which defines conciseness is an important metric and has influence on the other metrics. When the summary is nil it has maximum information loss and when conciseness is nil, the summary contains the whole dataset has no information loss. So, the information loss and conciseness are orthogonal. In our experiments, we used five different summary sizes to evaluate summarization results. Although, the summary size is decided by the network manager/analyst based on the network, in future we will explore to find the optimal summary size without user input. Tables 5 and 6 displays the summarization results based on the metrics discussed above. It is not surprising that, the conciseness and interestingness remain same for both the approaches. As stated earlier, summary size defines conciseness and we used the same summary size for both approaches.

Table 5. Results on KDD Cup dataset

Summary size	Conciseness		Information loss		Interestingness		Intelligibility	
	FIBS	NTS	FIBS	NTS	FIBS	NTS	FIBS	NTS
10	200	**200**	0.97	**0.91**	0.15	**0.15**	0.22	**1.0**
20	100	**100**	0.96	**0.89**	0.06	**0.06**	0.25	**1.0**
30	66.67	**66.67**	0.96	**0.88**	0.04	**0.04**	0.27	**1.0**
40	50	**50**	0.94	**0.85**	0.03	**0.03**	0.29	**1.0**
50	40	**40**	0.92	**0.81**	0.04	**0.04**	0.32	**1.0**

*FIBS = Feature-wise Intersection based Summarization, NTS = Network Traffic Summarization.

Table 6. Results on labelled TCP dataset

Summary size	Conciseness		Information loss		Interestingness		Intelligibility	
	FIBS	NTS	FIBS	NTS	FIBS	NTS	FIBS	NTS
10	257.5	**257.5**	0.99	**0.97**	0.13	**0.13**	0.18	**1.0**
20	128.75	**128.75**	0.99	**0.97**	0.05	**0.05**	0.18	**1.0**
30	85.83	**85.83**	0.99	**0.96**	0.04	**0.04**	0.19	**1.0**
40	64.375	**64.375**	0.98	**0.94**	0.03	**0.03**	0.20	**1.0**
50	51.5	**51.5**	0.98	**0.93**	0.02	**0.02**	0.21	**1.0**

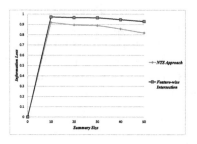

Fig. 1. Information loss on KDD cup dataset

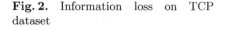

Fig. 2. Information loss on TCP dataset

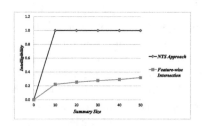

Fig. 3. Intelligibility on KDD cup dataset

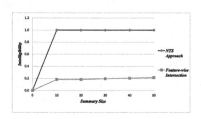

Fig. 4. Intelligibility on TCP dataset

Also, interestingness remains the same, because interestingness considers number of tuples in a summary and total number of input data points both of which are identical for the two approaches.

Figures 1 and 2 show the information loss of the proposed approach and the feature-wise intersection based approach. In both the cases, it is visible that, our proposed approach has lower information loss than the other approach, which reflects the strength of our technique based on the k-$medoid$ clustering algorithm. Figures 3 and 4 display the intelligibility and it is found that our proposed approach outperforms feature-wise intersection based approach, since the proposed NTS algorithm represents the original data instances in the summary.

5   Conclusion

In this paper, we proposed a new definition for clustering based network traffic summary which outperforms the existing feature-wise intersection based summary. We presented an algorithm which has the ability to handle categorical data in the summarization process. We experimented with widely used KDD cup dataset and also real life network traffic including simulated attacks. We used the most recently proposed summarization metrics to evaluate our results. We also propose a metric to evaluate summaries when other metric values are identical. In future, we will investigate frequent itemset based summarization process and will focus on real-time network traffic summarization along with finding the optimal summary size without user input.

References

1. Hoplaros, D., Tari, Z., Khalil, I.: Data summarization for network traffic monitoring. J. Netw. Comput. Appl. **37**, 194–205 (2014)
2. Wang, X., Abraham, A., Smith, K.A.: Intelligent web traffic mining and analysis. J. Netw. Compu. Appl. **28**(2), 147–165 (2005)
3. Keys, K., Moore, D., Estan, C.: A robust system for accurate real-time summaries of internet traffic. In: Proceedings of the 2005 ACM SIGMETRICS International Conference on Measurement and Modeling of Computer Systems, SIGMETRICS 2005, pp. 85–96. ACM, New York (2005)
4. Mahmood, A., Leckie, C., Udaya, P.: A scalable sampling scheme for clustering in network traffic analysis. In: Proceedings of the 2nd International Conference on Scalable Information Systems, InfoScale 2007, pp. 38:1–38 (2007)
5. Ahmed M., Naser, A.: Clustering based saemantic data summarization technique: a new approach. In: Accepted to appear in 9th IEEE Conference on Industrial Electronics and Applications (ICIEA), China (2014)
6. MacQueen, J.B.: Some methods for classification and analysis of multivariate observations. In: Cam, L.M.L., Neyman, J. (eds.) Proceedings of the Fifth Berkeley Symposium on Mathematical Statistics and Probability, vol. 1, pp. 281–297. University of California Press (1967)
7. Chandola, V., Kumar, V.: Summarization - compressing data into an informative representation. Knowl. Inf. Syst. **12**(3), 355–378 (2007)
8. Wendel, P., Ghanem, M., Guo, Y.: Scalable clustering on the data grid. In: 5th IEEE International Symposium Cluster Computing and the Grid (CCGrid) (2005)
9. More P., Hall, L.: Scalable clustering: a distributed approach. In: Proceedings of the 2004 IEEE International Conference on Fuzzy Systems, vol. 1, pp. 143–148 (2004)
10. Kendall, K.: A database of computer attacks for the evaluation of intrusion detection systems. In: Proceedings of DARPA Information Survivality Conference and Eexposition (DISCEX), DARPA Off-line Intrusion Detection Evaluation, pp. 12–26 (1999)
11. 1999 kdd cup dataset. http://www.kdd.ics.uci.edu

12. Leung, K., Leckie, C.: Unsupervised anomaly detection in network intrusion detection using clusters. In: Proceedings of the Twenty-Eighth Australasian Conference on Computer Science, ACSC 2005, vol. 38, pp. 333–342. Australian Computer Society Inc., Darlinghurst (2005)
13. Shafi, K., Abbass, H.: Evaluation of an adaptive genetic-based signature extraction system for network intrusion detection. Pattern Anal. Appl. **16**(4), 549–566 (2013)
14. The Fully Labelled TCP dataset. http://seit.unsw.adfa.edu.au/staff/sites/kshafi/Datasets

Heart Disease Diagnosis Using Co-clustering

Mohiuddin Ahmed[✉], Abdun Naser Mahmood, and Michael J. Maher

School of Engineering and Information Technology, UNSW Canberra,
Canberra, ACT 2600, Australia
Mohiuddin.Ahmed@student.unsw.edu.au,
{A.Mahmood,M.Maher}@unsw.edu.au

Abstract. Due to the advancement of information technology and its incorporation in various health applications, a huge amount of medical data is being produced continuously. Consequently, efficient techniques are required to analyse such large datasets and extract meaningful information as well as knowledge. Disease diagnosis is an important application domain of data mining techniques and can be resembled with the anomaly detection which is one of the primary tasks of data mining research. In past decades, heart disease caused the maximum death all over the world. As a result, heart disease diagnosis is a challenge for both data mining and health care communities. In this paper, co-clustering is introduced as a powerful data analysis tool to diagnose heart disease and extract the underlying data pattern of the datasets. The performance of the proposed method is evaluated using Cleveland Clinic Foundation Heart Disease dataset against other existing clustering based anomaly detection techniques. Experimental results reflect not only better accuracy but also meaningful information about the dataset which is helpful for further analysis of heart disease diagnosis.

Keywords: Scalable data mining · Co-clustering · Heart disease diagnosis

1 Introduction

According to World Health Organization, heart disease is the leading cause of death around the world in past decades [1,16]. Since, the mortality rate of heart disease patients are increasing every year, data mining community is interested in extracting useful knowledge from the huge amount of patients data available. Medical and healthcare domain has attracted significant interest from data mining and machine learning research community. In this domain, the data mining techniques try to solve the problems which are most significant because of human lives involvement. Application of different data mining techniques are already in practise for several diseases like cancer, diabetics and heart disease [4].

Anomaly detection is an important aspect of data mining, where the main objective is to identify anomalous or unusual data from a given dataset. Anomaly detection is interesting because it involves automatically discovering interesting

© Institute for Computer Sciences, Social Informatics and Telecommunications Engineering 2015
J. Jung et al. (Eds.): INFOSCALE 2014, LNICST 139, pp. 61–70, 2015.
DOI: 10.1007/978-3-319-16868-5_6

and rare patterns from datasets. Anomaly detection has been widely studied in statistics and machine learning, also known as outlier detection, deviation detection, novelty detection, and exception mining [3]. In the scope of this paper, anomaly can be considered as sick people as well as having heart disease. Clustering, which groups together similar data instances is a type of anomaly detection schemes and has been applied to solve different problems [2].

In this paper, we introduce a set of emerging data mining and machine learning algorithms to solve the problem of identifying abnormal instances from heart disease datasets as well as identifying sick people along with extracting useful knowledge. We propose to use co-clustering, which finds subsets of rows in the data that are correlated with a subset of its columns [8,9]. Co-clustering is unlike the regular clustering which only performs one way clustering such as *k-means* [5]. Co-clustering can be considered as simultaneous clustering of both row and column instances. In this paper, we utilize the co-clustering algorithms to solve the heart disease diagnosis problem as well as finding the underlying data pattern.

The roadmap of this paper is organized as follows: Sect. 2 provides a discussion on clustering based anomaly detection techniques followed by co-clustering in Sect. 3. Section 4 contains brief description of the dataset used in this paper and experimental results in detail. We conclude our paper stating the future research directions in Sect. 5.

2   Anomaly Detection Techniques and Related Works

In this section, we highlight few clustering based as well as distance based anomaly detection techniques. We compare our proposed method with the techniques discussed in this section.

Knorr et al [10] presented the algorithms to detect distance-based outliers. They consider a data point O in a dataset T, a $DB(p;D)$-outlier, if at least a fraction p of the data points in T lies greater than distance D from O. Their index-based algorithm executes a range search with radius D for each data point. If the number of data points in its D-*neighborhood* exceeds a threshold, the search stops and that data point is declared as a non-outlier, otherwise it is an outlier. This concept is further extended my Ramaswamy et al [11] where the anomaly score is based on the k-*nearest neighbor* implementation.

Breunig et al [12] proposed an idea to assign each object a degree of being outlier. This degree is called Local Outlier Factor (LOF). LOF depends on how isolated the object is with respect to the surrounding neighbourhood. The local outlier factor of an object p is caclualted using the following Eq. (1)

$$LOF_{MinPts}(p) = \frac{\sum_{o \in N_{MinPts}(p)} \frac{lrd_{MinPts}(o)}{lrd_{MinPts}(p)}}{|N_{MinPts}(p)|} \tag{1}$$

This outlier factor of object p calculates the degree to which p can be called as outlier. Outlier factor is the average of the ratio of the local reachability density of p and those of ps MinPts-nearest neighbours. The author also described mathematically the LOF for objects deep in a cluster along with general bounds (upper, lower, and tight). The impact of MinPts to calculate LOF is also elaborated with necessary examples. Their approach can intelligently choose the range of k; the LOF approach has lower computational complexity than the depth-based approaches for large dimensionality.

He et al [13] proposed a definition for cluster based local anomalies. According to their definition, all the data points in a certain cluster are considered as anomalies rather than a single point, as shown in Fig. 1. The clusters C1 and C3 are considered as anomalous. They used some numeric parameters, i.e. α, β to identify Small Cluster (SC) and Large Cluster (LC). The clustering technique depends on these parameters but it is not clear how the values can be determined for various datasets. They used the SQUEEZER algorithm to cluster data, as it achieves both high quality of clustering and can handle high dimensional data. Then the FindCBLOF algorithm determines outlier factor of each individual record in dataset. $CBLOF(t)$ for each record t is calculated following Eq. (2):

$$CBLOF(t) = \begin{cases} |C_i| * min(d(t, C_j)) \ where \ t \in C_i, C_i \in SC \\ \qquad and \ C_j \in LC \ for \ j = 1 \ to \ b \\ |C_i| * (d(t, C_i)) \ where \ t \in C_i \\ \qquad and \ C_i \in LC \end{cases} \qquad (2)$$

Amer et al [14] introduced Local Density Cluster-Based Outlier Factor (LDC-OF) which can be considered as a variant of CBLOF [13]. The LDCOF score (6) is calculated as the distance to the nearest large cluster divided by the average distance to the cluster center of the elements in that large cluster. LDCOF score will be **A** when $p \in C_i \in SC$ where $C_j \in LC$ and **B** when $p \in C_i \in LC$

$$distance_{avg}(C) = \frac{\sum_{i \in C} d(i, C)}{|C|} \qquad (3)$$

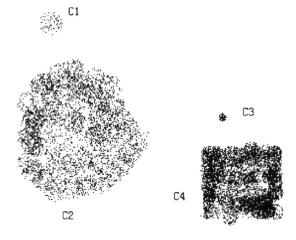

Fig. 1. Anomalous clusters C1,C3; adapted from [13]

$$A = \frac{min(d(p, C_j))}{distance_{avg}(C_j)} \qquad (4)$$

$$B = \frac{d(p, C_i)}{distance_{avg}(C_i)} \qquad (5)$$

$$LDCOF(p) = A \mid B; \qquad (6)$$

3   Co-clustering

Co-clustering can be simply considered as a simultaneous clustering of both rows and columns. Co-clustering can produce a set of **c** column clusters of the original columns **C** and a set of **r** row clusters of original row instances **R** [6]. Unlike other clustering algorithms, co-clustering also defines a clustering criterion and then optimizes it. In a nutshell, co-clustering finds out the subsets of rows and columns simultaneously of a data matrix using a specified criterion. From the summarization point of view, co-clustering provides significant benefits. The following Fig. 2 shows the original dataset **D** and the summary of **sD**. The original data has four attributes and these are of two categories. The original row instances of the dataset contain two types of data as normal and anomalous. So, the motivation behind using co-clustering is that, co-clustering can be able to produce clusters to represent the underlying data pattern in a concise form yet without losing any information of the original data.

Next, we discuss the basics of co-clustering algorithms within the scope of this paper. We will mainly focus on block co-clustering and information theoretic co-clustering [9].

3.1   Block Co-clustering

Govaert and Nadif et al. [7] proposed a probabilistic framework for model based co-clustering. The backbone of their proposed block co-clustering is latent block model. This model is based on the conditional independence and independent latent variables. For a given matrix **x** of two dimensions as row **R** and column **C**, the existence of partition **z** on **R** and partition **w** on **C** is assumed in a way that the univariate random variables x_{rc} are conditionally independent knowing **z** and **w** with a parameterized pdf $f(x_{rc}; \alpha_{kl})$, when the row **r** belongs to the cluster **k** and column **c** belong to the cluster **l**. Thus the conditional pdf of x, knowing **z** and **w** can be termed as follows

$$\prod_{r,c} f(x_{r,c}; \alpha_{z_r w_c}) = \prod_{r,c,k,l} \{f(x_{rc}; \alpha_{kl})\}^{z_{rk} w_{cl}} \qquad (7)$$

The latent variables as $z_1, \ldots, z_n, w_1, \ldots, w_d$ are considered to be independent as follows

$$p(z, w) = p(z)p(w), p(z) = \prod_r p(z_r) \ and \ p(w) = \prod_c p(w_c) \qquad (8)$$

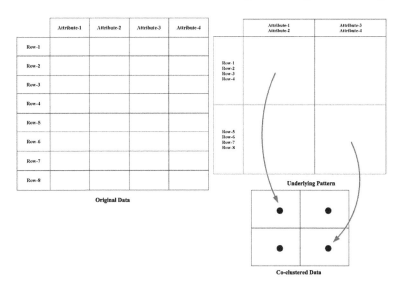

Fig. 2. Co-clustering and summarization

Consequently, the parameters of latent block model become $\theta = (\pi, \rho, \alpha)$. Where $\pi = (\pi_1, ..., \pi_g)$ and $\rho = (\rho_1, ..., \rho_m)$ and $(\pi_k = P(z_{rk=1}, k = 1, ..., g))$, $(\rho_l = P(w_{cl=1}, l = 1, ..., m))$ are the mixing proportions. And α_{kl} is the parameter of the distribution of block **k,l**. Now, if **Z** and **W** are denoted as the possible labels **z** for **R** and **c** for **C**, the pdf of original data **x** can be represented as follows

$$f(x; \theta) = \sum_{(z,w) \in Z \times W} p(z, w) f(x|z, w; \theta)$$

$$= \sum_{(z,w) \in Z \times W} \prod_{r,k} \pi_k^{z_{rk}} \prod_{c,l} \rho_l^{w_{cl}} \prod_{r,c,k,l} \{f(x_{rc}; \alpha_{kl})\}^{z_{rk} w_{cl}} \tag{9}$$

To derive the maximum likelihood estimate of θ, two types of expectation maximization approach can be used such as variational EM and classification EM. For a latent block model, **R** is a distribution on $Z \times W$ and $\mathbf{R} = P(z,w|x,\theta)$. Here, we discuss only classification EM approach, where the objective is to maximize the classification log-likelihood (10).

$$L_c(z, w; \theta) = \sum_{r,k} z_{rk} log \pi_k + \sum_{c,l} w_{cl} log \rho_l + \sum_{r,c,k,l} z_{rk} w_{cl} f(x_{rc}, \alpha_{kl}) \tag{10}$$

The corresponding latent block classification EM algorithm is presented in the *Algorithm* below.

3.2 Information Theoretic Co-clustering

Banerjee et al. [9] proposed information theoretic co-clustering based on *Bregman Divergence*. It tries to minimize the information loss in the approximation of

---

Algorithm: Latent Block Classification Expectation Maximization (LBCEM)

Input: x,g,m.

Initialization: z,w, $\pi_k = \frac{z_k}{n}, \rho_l = \frac{w_l}{d}, \alpha_{kl} = arg\ max_{\alpha kl} \sum_{r,c} z_{rk} w_{cl} log\ f(x_{rc}, \alpha_{kl})$

repeat

  repeat

    Step 1: $z_r = argmax_k(\sum_{c,l} w_{cl} log\ f(x_{rc}, \alpha_{kl}) + log\ \pi_k)$

    Step 2: $\pi_k = \frac{z_k}{n}, \alpha_{kl} = arg\ max_{\alpha kl} \sum_{r,c} z_{rk} w_{cl} log\ f(x_{rc}, \alpha_{kl})$

  until convergence

  repeat

    Step 3: $w_c = argmax_l(\sum_{r,k} z_{rk} log\ f(x_{rc}, \alpha_{kl}) + log\ \rho_l)$

    Step 4: $\rho_l = \frac{\widetilde{w}_l}{d}, \alpha_{kl} = argmax_{\alpha kl} \sum_{r,c} z_{rk} w_{cl} log\ f(x_{rc}, \alpha_{kl})$

  until convergence

until convergence

return π, ρ, α, z, w

---

a data matrix $\mathbf{X}$, in terms of a predefined bregman divergence function. For a given co-clustering $(\mathbf{R},\mathbf{C})$ and a matrix approximation scheme $\mathbf{M}$, a class of random variables which store the characteristics of data matrix $\mathbf{X}$ is defined. The objective function tries to minimize the information loss on the approximation of $\widetilde{X}$ for a co-clustering $\mathbf{R},\mathbf{C}$. The Bregman information of $\mathbf{X}$ can be defined as follows

$$I_\phi(X) = E\left[log\left(\frac{X}{E[X]}\right)\right] \tag{11}$$

Here, the matrix approximation scheme is defined by the expected value and the bregman divergence d_ϕ for an optimal co-clustering as follows

$$(R^*, C^*) = arg\ min\ E[d_\phi(X, \widetilde{X})] \tag{12}$$

Here, d_ϕ, can be considered in two ways as follows.

$$\mathbf{I - Divergence} :d_\phi(x_1, x_2) = x_1 log(\frac{x_1}{x_2}) - (x_1 - x_2) \tag{13}$$

$$\mathbf{EuclideanDistance} :: d_\phi(x_1, x_2) = (x_1 - x_2)^2 \tag{14}$$

4   Experimental Analysis

In this section, we apply two different co-clustering algorithm discussed earlier for the disease diagnosis. At first, we give a brief description of the dataset used and then we discuss the experimental results in Sect. 4.2.

4.1   Heart Disease Dataset

The datset used in this paper is available in UCI Machine Learning Repository [15]. The dataset contains 76 attributes; however for experimental purpose only 13 of them are used. Instances with missing values are removed from the dataset. Table 1 contains short description on the dataset [16].

Table 1. Cleveland heart disease dataset attributes

Name	Data Type	Description
Age	Continuous	Age in years
Sex	Discrete	Male/Female
Cp	Discrete	Chest pain type
Trestbps	Continuous	Resting blood pressure
Chol	Continuous	Serum cholesterol in mg/dl
Fbs	Discrete	Fasting blood sugar
Restecg	Discrete	Resting electrocardiographic results
Thalach	Continuous	Maximum heart rate achieved
Exang	Discrete	Exercise induced angina
Old Peak ST	Continuous	Depression induced by exercise relative to rest
Slope	Discrete	The slope of peak exercise segment
Ca	Discrete	Number of major vessels colored by fluroscopy that ranged between 0 and 3
Thal	Discrete	Normal, Fixed defect, Reversible defect

Table 2. Standard confusion metrics for evaluation of co-clustering algorithm

Actual Diagnosis	Healthy	Sick
Healthy	TN	FP
Sick	FN	TP

4.2 Result Analysis

We applied co-clustering techniques with the input (*Row=2, Column=2*). Since, our aim to identify the sick people and healthy people and it is expected that two cluster will reflect the underlying data pattern. For the columns, we also wanted to identify, which attributes contribute more for identifying sick people as well as anomalous instances. Once we have the co-clustering results, we analyse the clusters produced to calculate the accuracy of the underlying data pattern accuracy as well whether the co-clustering is able to detect sick people accurately (Table 2).

We measure the accuracy of our approach using the standard confusion metrics. The metrics are listed as True Positive (TP), False Positive (FP), True Negative (TN), False negative (FN). Table 4 displays the confusion metrics.

- TP = Sick people correctly identified as sick.
- FP = Healthy people incorrectly identified as sick.
- TN = Healthy people correctly identified as healthy.
- FN = Sick people incorrectly identified as healthy.

The accuracy is computed using Eq. (15)

$$Accuracy = \frac{TP + TN}{TP + TN + FP + FN} \tag{15}$$

Table 3. Performance evaluation on Heart Disease Dataset [15]

Techniques	Accuracy on Heart Disease Data [15]
KNN	**58 %**
LOF	**52 %**
CBLOF	**43 %**
LDCOF	**49 %**
Block Co-clustering	**71 %**
Information Theoretic Co-clustering	**76 %**

Table 4. Information Theoretic Co-clustering on Heart Disease Dataset [15]

Actual Diagnosis	Healthy	Sick
	Fbs, Exang, Old Peak ST, Ca, Thal	**Age, Sex, Cp, Trestbps, Chol, Restecg, Thlach, Slope**
Cluster-1	120	32
Cluster-2	40	105

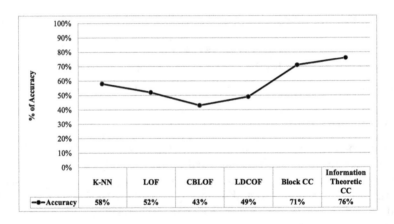

Fig. 3. Performance of different techniques for heart disease diagnosis

The results were compared against KNN [11], LOF [12], CBLOF [13], LDCOF [14] techniques. Table 3 displays the accuracy comparison results and it is clear that, the application of co-clustering for heart disease diagnosis outperforms the existing anomaly detection techniques. Among the co-clustering techniques, information theoretic co-clustering performs better than the block co-clustering.

Table 4 shows the co-clustering results of the information theoretic co-clustering in detail. It is also clear that, there are few attributes which contribute more to represent the sick/abnormal instances. So, further emphasis can be given by the health care professionals to diagnose more precisely in future. Figure 3 graphically represent the accuracy comparison of the various techniques.

5   Conclusion

In this paper, we have raised the issue of handling huge amount of medical data and extracting useful knowledge from the data. Apart from the regular anomaly detection techniques, we have incorporated the co-clustering techniques, which are emerging set of algorithms in data mining and machine learning. Experimental results show that, the information theoretic co-clustering can diagnose the heart disease data better than the other clustering based anomaly detection techniques as well as the block co-clustering. In future, we will focus on creating concise yet informative summary from the medical datasets to help healthcare professionals to enhance the treatment facilities.

References

1. World Health Organization. http://www.who.int/en/
2. Chandola, V., Banerjee, A.: Anomaly detection: a survey. ACM Comput. Surv. **41**(3), 15:1–15:58 (2009)
3. Ahmed, M., Mahmood, A., Hu, J.: Outlier detection. In: Khan Pathan, A.-S. (ed.) The State of the Art in Intrusion Prevention and Detection, pp. 3–23. CRC Press, Boca Raton (2014)
4. Fang, X.: Are you becoming a diabetic? a data mining approach. In: Proceedings of the 6th International Conference on Fuzzy Systems and Knowledge Discovery - Volume 5, ser. FSKD 2009, pp. 18–22. IEEE Press, Piscataway (2009)
5. Ahmed. M., Naser. A.: A novel approach for outlier detection and clustering improvement. In: 2013 8th IEEE Conference on Industrial Electronics and Applications (ICIEA), pp. 577–582 (2013)
6. Tucker, L.R.: The extension of factor analysis to three-dimensional matrices. In: Gulliksen, H., Frederiksen, N. (eds.) Contributions to Mathematical Psychology, pp. 110–127. Holt, Rinehart and Winston, New York (1964)
7. Tucker, L.R.: Clustering with block mixture models. Pattern Recogn. **36**(2), 463–473 (2003)
8. Tucker, L.R.: Block clustering with bernoulli mixture models: comparison of different approaches. Comput. Stat. Data Anal. **52**(6), 3233–3245 (2008)
9. Banerjee, A., Dhillon, I., Ghosh, J., Merugu, S., Modha, D.S.: A generalized maximum entropy approach to bregman co-clustering and matrix approximation. J. Mach. Learn. Res. **8**, 1919–1986 (2007)
10. Knorr, E.M., Ng, R.T.: Algorithms for mining distance-based outliers in large datasets. In: Proceedings of the 24rd International Conference on Very Large Data Bases, ser. VLDB 1998, pp. 392–403. Morgan Kaufmann Publishers Inc., San Francisco (1998)
11. Ramaswamy, S., Rastogi, R., Shim, K.: Efficient algorithms for mining outliers from large data sets. SIGMOD Rec. **29**(2), 427–438 (2000)
12. Breunig, M.M., Kriegel, H.-P., Ng, R.T., Sander, J.: Lof: identifying density-based local outliers. SIGMOD Rec. **29**(2), 93–104 (2000)
13. He, Z., Xu, X., Deng, S.: Discovering cluster based local outliers. Pattern Recogn. Lett. **2003**, 9–10 (2003)
14. Mennatallah Amer, M.G.: Nearest-neighbor and Clustering Based Anomaly Detection Algorithms For Rapidminer. Shaker Verlag GmbH, Aachen (2012)

15. Bache, K., Lichman, M.: UCI machine learning repository (2013). http://archive.ics.uci.edu/ml
16. Shouman, M., Turner, T., Stocker, R.: Using decision tree for diagnosing heart disease patients. In: Proceedings of the Ninth Australasian Data Mining Conference - Volume 121, ser. AusDM 2011, pp. 23–30. Australian Computer Society Inc., Darlinghurst (2011)

An Investigation of Scalable Anomaly Detection Techniques for a Large Network of Wi-Fi Hotspots

Pheeha Machaka[1(✉)] and Antoine Bagula[2]

[1] Council for Scientific and Industrial Research Modelling and Digital Science, Meiring Naude Rd, Pretoria 0184, South Africa
pmachaka@csir.co.za
[2] University of the Western Cape, Robert Sobukwe Road, Bellville 7535, South Africa
bbagula@uwc.ac.za

Abstract. The paper seeks to investigate the use of scalable machine learning techniques to address anomaly detection problem in a large Wi-Fi network. This was in the efforts of achieving a highly scalable preemptive monitoring tool for wireless networks. The Neural Networks, Bayesian Networks and Artificial Immune Systems were used for this experiment. Using a set of data extracted from a live network of Wi-Fi hotspots managed by an ISP; we integrated algorithms into a data collection system to detect anomalous performance over several test case scenarios. The results are revealed and discussed in terms of both anomaly performance and statistical significance.

Keywords: Performance monitoring · Neural networks · Artificial immune systems · Bayesian networks · Anomaly performance detection · Multilayer perceptron · Naive bayes · AIRS2

1 Introduction

Wireless Fidelity (Wi-Fi) is a wireless networking technology that uses radio waves to provide high-speed wireless internet connections. Wi-Fi is based on the IEEE 802.11 standards and builds upon a fast, easy and inexpensive networking approach [1] where Access Points (APs) are used to broadcast signals to Wi-Fi-capable client devices (laptops and Smartphone devices) within their range, and connect to the Internet.

Performance monitoring is an important task upon which large Wi-Fi network deployment depends. As traditionally implemented, performance monitoring is based on a reactive network approach where the operating system software only warns the network administrators when a problem occurs. This approach leads to both the halting of important network processes and the hampering of critical business processes of the organization.

Pre-emptive network monitoring provides the potential to prevent the occurrence of faults by analyzing the status of the network components to create a fail-safe network status or allow a smooth migration from a faulty to fail-safe network status. Wi-Fi

© Institute for Computer Sciences, Social Informatics and Telecommunications Engineering 2015
J. Jung et al. (Eds.): INFOSCALE 2014, LNICST 139, pp. 71–79, 2015.
DOI: 10.1007/978-3-319-16868-5_7

technology has become so popular and this lead to large scale deployment of thousands of hotspots networks. These hotspots generate huge amounts of monitoring data, thus there is a call for efficient data handling methods that would analyze data and recognize anomalous hidden patterns and implement fault tolerance mechanism. While statistical analysis methods have been deployed in many cases to address this issue, soft computing methods borrowed from the human immune system are emerging as powerful tools used in anomaly detection and security monitoring systems.

1.1 Related Work

There has been work done in the field of anomaly detection, and in this paper, three soft computing methods were identified, viz. Artificial Neural Networks, Artificial Immune Systems and Bayesian Networks. With Artificial Neural Network (ANN), the work has focused on employing ANN for anomaly detection on network traffic data [2–4]. Artificial Immune Systems (AIS) was used for intrusion detection, and detection of computer viruses [5–7].Bayesian Networks were also used for anomaly detection for disease outbreak [4] and also in detecting and analyzing anomaly behavior in network-based FTP services [8].

The three machine learning techniques have gained success in anomaly detection and in this paper; we would like to employ them on a large network of Wi-Fi hotspots for intrusion detection. The work done in this paper furthers the work by authors in [9–11] and the efforts to find out which method works best for large data networks, and how each methods performs under network intrusion for the test cases set out in this paper.

1. Which method performs better for monitoring a large Wi-Fi network?
2. How do these methods perform under different test cases and network thresholds?

The remainder of the paper is organized as follows: in Sect. 2, the machine learning techniques used in this article are briefly described. Section 3 will describe the research and experiment design. Section 4 will reveal and discuss the experiment results while Sect. 5 brings the article to a conclusion.

2 Algorithms

Artificial Neural Networks - ANN's are mathematical or computational models that get their inspiration from biological neural systems. In this paper the neural network model, Multilayer Perceptron (MLP) was used to conduct experiments. The MLP is a feed forward neural network model in which vertices are arranged in layers. MLP have one or more layer(s) of hidden nodes, which are not directly connected to the input and output nodes [12]. For the purpose of this experiment we employed Weka's Multilayer Perceptron implementation.

Bayesian Networks - Bayesian Networks can be described briefly as acyclic directed graph (DAG) which defines a factorisation of a joint probability distribution over the variables that are represented by the nodes of the DAG, where the factorisation is given by the direct links of the DAG [13]. The NaiveBayes algorithm was used for the experiments. It makes a strong assumption that all attributes of the examples are independent of each other given the context of the class. The Weka's NaiveBayes implements this probabilistic Naïve Bayes classifier [14].

Artificial Immune Systems - The AIS takes inspiration from the robust and powerful capabilities of the Human Immune System's (HIS) capabilities to distinguish between self and non-self [7]. The Algorithm employed in this paper's experiments is the Weka's Artificial Immune Recognition System (AIRS) learning algorithm [15]. The AIRS is a supervised AIS learning algorithm that has shown significant success on a broad range of classification problems [5–7].

3   The Research Design

The section that follows will describe the methods and techniques used to carry out the research presented in this paper.

3.1   The Wi-Fi Network

The experiment network connected more than 400 hotspots around the Cape Town area, with more than 615 Cisco WRT54GL gateway devices connected to the network. For data collection and monitoring, a Syslog daemon program was installed on each gateway device, and was left to run 2–3 months collecting monitoring data at every hour's interval.

3.2   Network Performance Monitoring

The network was monitored based on three performance metrics. This includes:

- Uptime and Downtime (%) - This metric measures the availability, stability and reliability of the communication device when used in the network.
- Load Average (%) - Measures the "congestion rate" for the device based on the number of users connected to the device.
- Radio Noise (in dB) - Wi-Fi uses the shared 2.4 GHz spectrum band and the proliferation of devices using the spectrum leads to congestion and noisy Wi-Fi devices.
- Standard deviation - To detect aberrant behavior in performance, statistical confidence bands were used to measure deviations in a time series. A deviation depends on the Delta (δ) parameter whose sensible values were taken between 0 and 3.
- Encoding and Selection - Three levels of performance were used to describe performance. A 3-bit encoded nominal value was used to describe performance. This type of encoding was also used by authors in [11].

3.3   Performance Evaluation Techniques

The effectiveness of the methods is evaluated based on their ability to make correct predictions. The following measures were used to quantify the performance of the algorithms:

- True Positive (TP) rate, also known as detection rate.
- False Positive (FP) rate, also known as false alarm rate.
- F-measure, it is a harmonic mean for precision and recall.
- Kappa Statistic - used to measure the agreement between predicted and observed categorization of a dataset, while correcting for agreement that occurs by chance.

3.4 Test Cases

For the test cases in this study, we followed a model suggested by the authors in [92-Wu Shelly]. We conducted experiments using four test case scenarios revealing Wi-Fi operating constraints from loose (e.g. rural setting where QoS is an issue) to the most stringent (e.g. Suburban setting where modern applications demand higher QoS).

The Weka machine learning software was used for the experiments, a stratified 10-fold cross-validation technique was used for training and testing the algorithms.

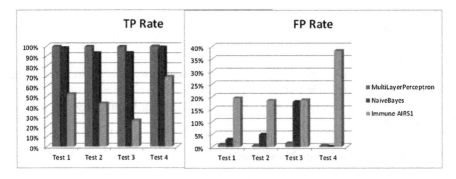

Fig. 1. Anomaly TP rate and FP rate performance

4 Results and Discussions

Using the test cases and methods described above; the experiments were conducted and results were revealed based on the algorithms': True Positive (TP), False Positive (FP), Kappa Statistic and F-measure performance. A graphical and t-test performance evaluation is used.

4.1 True Positive Rate Performance

In the bar graph representation of Fig. 1 above indicates a bar graph representation of TP rate and that the MLP had an average TP rate of 99.45 %, while NaiveBayes had an average TP rate of 95.62 % across all test cases. The AIRS1 algorithm's performance was lower in recognising classes correctly with average TP rate of 47.65 %.

For the test:

$$\begin{aligned}
\text{True Positive Rate: } & H_0: \mu_{\text{MLP}} - \mu_{\text{NaiveBayes}} = 0 \\
\text{True Positive Rate: } & H_1: \mu_{\text{MLP}} - \mu_{\text{NaiveBayes}} \neq 0
\end{aligned} \tag{1}$$

Table 1. Results for true positive rate T-test for paired two samples for means

	Multilayer Perceptron	NaiveBayes		Multilayer Perceptron	AIRS2
Mean	0.9810	0.9563	Mean	0.9810	0.4519
Variance	0.0001	0.0007	Variance	0.0001	0.0524
Observations	200	200	Observations	200	200
Hypothesised Mean Difference	0		Hypothesised Mean Difference	0	
t Stat	13.8587		t Stat	32.9818	
P(T<=t) two tailed	0.0000		P(T<=t) two tailed	0.0000	

In Table 1, the value of the t-Statistic is 13.858 and its two-tailed p-value is 5.147E-31. At the 5 % confidence level, the test is highly significant and there is overwhelming evidence to infer that the alternative hypothesis is true. Therefore we reject the null hypothesis and conclude that there is a difference in the mean anomaly True Positive Rate for the MLP and NaiveBayes algorithms.

For the test:

$$\text{True Positive Rate: } H_0: \mu_{\text{MLP}} - \mu_{\text{AIRS2}} = 0$$
$$\text{True Positive Rate: } H_1: \mu_{\text{MLP}} - \mu_{\text{AIRS2}} \neq 0 \tag{2}$$

The value of the t-Statistic is 32.981 and its two-tailed p-value is 1.34191E-82. At the 5 % confidence level, the test is highly significant and there is overwhelming evidence to infer that the alternative hypothesis is true. Therefore we reject the null hypothesis and conclude that there is a difference in the mean anomaly True Positive Rate for the MLP and AIRS2 algorithms.

4.2 False Positive Rate Performance

The bar graph representation in Fig. 1 indicates that the MLP and NaiveBayes had very low average FP rate, 0.77 % and 6.45 % respectively. A poor performance was seen with AIRS1 technique; it had an average FP rate of 23.65 %, and had a high FP rate of 38.2 % in test case 4.

For the test:

$$\text{False Positive Rate: } H_0: \mu_{\text{MLP}} - \mu_{\text{NaiveBayes}} = 0$$
$$\text{False Positive Rate: } H_1: \mu_{\text{MLP}} - \mu_{\text{NaiveBayes}} \neq 0 \tag{3}$$

In Table 2 below, the value of the t-Statistic is -2.188 and its two-tailed p-value is 0.0298. At the 5 % confidence level, the test is significant and there is strong evidence to infer that the alternative hypothesis is true. Therefore we reject the null hypothesis and conclude that there is a difference in the mean anomaly False Positive Rate for the MLP and NaiveBayes algorithms.

For the test:

$$\text{False Positive Rate: } H_0: \mu_{\text{MLP}} - \mu_{\text{AIRS2}} = 0$$
$$\text{False Positive Rate: } H_1: \mu_{\text{MLP}} - \mu_{\text{AIRS2}} \neq 0 \tag{4}$$

Table 2. Results for false positive rate T-test for paired two samples for means

	Multilayer Perceptron	NaiveBayes		Multilayer Perceptron	AIRS2
Mean	0.0231	0.0301	Mean	0.0231	0.3507
Variance	0.0009	0.0012	Variance	0.0009	0.0407
Observations	200	200	Observations	200	200
Hypothesised Mean Difference	0		Hypothesised Mean Difference	0	
t Stat	-2.1882		t Stat	-22.4821	
P(T<=t) two tailed	0.0298		P(T<=t) two tailed	0.0000	

The value of the t-Statistic is -22.482 and its two-tailed p-value is 1.57884E-56. At the 5 % confidence level, the test is highly significant and there is overwhelming evidence to infer that the alternative hypothesis is true. Therefore we reject the null hypothesis and conclude that there is a difference in the mean anomaly False Positive Rate for the MLP and AIRS2 algorithms.

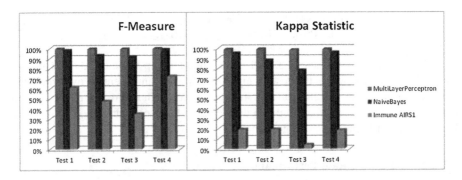

Fig. 2. Anomaly F-measure and Kappa statistic performance

4.3   F-Measure Performance

The MLP is shown to be, on average, the most accurate of the techniques with an average F-measure of 99.45 %. The NaiveBayes had an average F-measure of 95.25 % across all test cases. This is indicated by the bar graph representation in Fig. 2. AIRS1 revealed poor results with an average F-measure of 53.88 %.

Table 3. Results for F-measure T-test for paired two samples for means

	Multilayer Perceptron	NaiveBayes		Multilayer Perceptron	AIRS2
Mean	0.9804	0.9528	Mean	0.9804	0.4851
Variance	0.0001	0.0010	Variance	0.0001	0.0482
Observations	200	200	Observations	200	200
Hypothesised Mean Difference	0		Hypothesised Mean Difference	0	
t Stat	12.8538		t Stat	32.1631	
P(T<=t) two tailed	1.9720		P(T<=t) two tailed	0.0000	

For the test:

$$F - \text{Measure: } H_0: \mu_{\text{MLP}} - \mu_{\text{NaiveBayes}} = 0$$
$$F - \text{Measure: } H_1: \mu_{\text{MLP}} - \mu_{\text{NaiveBayes}} \neq 0 \tag{5}$$

The value of the t-Statistic is 12.853 and its two-tailed p-value is 6.32577E-28. At the 5 % confidence level, the test is highly significant and there is overwhelming evidence to infer that the alternative hypothesis is true. Therefore we reject the null hypothesis and conclude that there is a difference in the mean anomaly F-measure for the MLP and NaiveBayes algorithms.

For the test:

$$F - \text{Measure: } H_0: \mu_{\text{MLP}} - \mu_{\text{AIRS2}} = 0$$
$$F - \text{Measure: } H_1: \mu_{\text{MLP}} - \mu_{\text{AIRS2}} \neq 0 \tag{6}$$

The value of the t-Statistic is 32.163 and its two-tailed p-value is 9.08911E-81. At the 5 % confidence level, the test is highly significant and there is overwhelming evidence to infer that the alternative hypothesis is true. Therefore we reject the null hypothesis and conclude that there is a difference in the mean anomaly F-measure for the MLP and AIRS2 algorithms.

4.4   Kappa Statistic Performance

Indicated by the bar graph in Fig. 2, the MLP and NaiveBayes had an average Kappa statistic of 98.59 % and 89.05 %, respectively. AIRS1 technique had an average Kappa statistic of 15.22 %, revealing poor accuracy and precision.

Table 4. Results for Kappa statistic T-test for paired two samples for means

	Multilayer Perceptron	NaiveBayes		Multilayer Perceptron	AIRS2
Mean	0.9512	0.8906	Mean	0.9512	0.1551
Variance	0.0005	0.0052	Variance	0.0005	0.0157
Observations	200	200	Observations	200	200
Hypothesised Mean Difference	0		Hypothesised Mean Difference	0	
t Stat	12.5824		t Stat	91.0005	
P(T<=t) two tailed	1.9720		P(T<=t) two tailed	0.0000	

For the test:

$$\text{Kappa Statistic: } H_0: \mu_{\text{MLP}} - \mu_{\text{NaiveBayes}} = 0$$
$$\text{Kappa Statistic: } H_1: \mu_{\text{MLP}} - \mu_{\text{NaiveBayes}} \neq 0 \tag{7}$$

The value of the t-Statistic is 12.58 and its two-tailed p-value is 4.29687E-27. At the 5 % confidence level, the test is highly significant and there is overwhelming evidence to infer that the alternative hypothesis is true. Therefore we reject the null hypothesis and conclude that there is a difference in the mean anomaly Kappa Statistic for the MLP and NaiveBayes algorithms.

For the test:

$$\text{Kappa Statistic: } H_0: \mu_{MLP} - \mu_{AIRS2} = 0$$
$$\text{Kappa Statistic: } H_1: \mu_{MLP} - \mu_{AIRS2} \neq 0 \tag{8}$$

The value of the t-Statistic is 91.00 and its two-tailed p-value is 4.14E-164. At 5 % confidence level, the test is highly significant and there is overwhelming evidence to infer that the alternative hypothesis is true. Therefore we reject the null hypothesis and conclude that there is a difference in the mean anomaly Kappa Statistic for the MLP and AIRS2 algorithms.

5 Conclusions

The statistical hypothesis test experiments, Tables 1, 2, 3 and 4, that were conducted for anomaly performance detection reveal that, in all algorithm performance measures, there is a significant mean difference among the three algorithms. One can safely conclude that there was a significant difference in mean performance measures for MLP, NaiveBayes and the AIRS2 algorithms.

The bar chart representations in Figs. 1 and 2 were carefully examined, and for all performance measures, the MLP had an overall good performance and came out with the highest (above 90 %) algorithm performance measures. The NaiveBayes also had a good performance that was slightly lower than that of the MLP. On the other hand, the AIRS2 had a poor performance relative to the MLP and NaiveBayes.

When applying the algorithms to a large Wi-Fi networking problem, the MLP would be a better option as it would produce more accurate results. The NaiveBayes would also produce good results, but not better than that of the MLP. On the other hand, the AIRS2 algorithm may produce mediocre performance results on a large Wi-Fi network monitoring problem.

References

1. Vaughan-Nichols, S.J.: The challenge of wi-fi roaming. Computer **36**(7), 17–19 (2003)
2. Cannady, J.: Artificial neural networks for misuse detection. In: Presented at National Information Systems Security Conference (1998)
3. Cheng, E., Jin, H., Han, Z., Sun, J.: Network-based anomaly detection using an elman network. In: Lu, X., Zhao, W. (eds.) ICCNMC 2005. LNCS, vol. 3619, pp. 471–480. Springer, Heidelberg (2005)
4. Zhang, J., Zulkernine, M.: Anomaly based network intrusion detection with unsupervised outlier detection. In: Presented at IEEE International Conference On Communications, ICC 2006 (2006)

5. Forrest, S., Hofmeyr, S.A., Somayaji, A., Longstaff, T.A.: A sense of self for unix processes. In: Proceedings IEEE Symposium On Presented at Security and Privacy (1996)
6. Dasgupta, D., González, F.: An immunity-based technique to characterize intrusions in computer networks. IEEE Trans. Evol. Comput. **6**(3), 281–291 (2002)
7. Luther, K., Bye, R., Alpcan, T., Muller, A., Albayrak, S.: A cooperative AIS framework for intrusion detection. In: Presented at IEEE International Conference On Communications. ICC 2007 (2007)
8. Cha, B., Lee, D.: Network-based anomaly intrusion detection improvement by bayesian network and indirect relation. In: Apolloni, B., Howlett, R.J., Jain, L. (eds.) KES 2007, Part II. LNCS (LNAI), vol. 4693, pp. 141–148. Springer, Heidelberg (2007)
9. Machaka, P., Bagula, A., De Wet, N.: A highly scalable monitoring tool for wi-fi networks. In: Presented at 2012 IEEE 1st International Symposium On Wireless Systems (IDAACS-SWS) (2012)
10. Machaka, P., Bagula, A.: Preemptive performance monitoring of a large network of wi-fi hotspots: an artificial immune system. In: Masip-Bruin, X., Verchere, D., Tsaoussidis, V., Yannuzzi, M. (eds.) WWIC 2011. LNCS, vol. 6649, pp. 494–504. Springer, Heidelberg (2011)
11. Machaka, P., Mabande, T., Bagula, A.: Monitoring of a large wi-fi hotspots network: performance investigation of soft computing techniques. In: Hart, E., Timmis, J., Mitchell, P., Nakamo, T., Dabiri, F. (eds.) BIONETICS 2011. LNICST, vol. 103, pp. 155–162. Springer, Heidelberg (2012)
12. Dunne, R.A.: A Statistical Approach to Neural Networks for Pattern Recognition, vol. 702. Wiley, New York (2007)
13. Kjræulff, U.B., Madsen, A.L.: Bayesian Networks and Influence Diagrams: A Guide to Construction and Analysis, vol. 22. Springer, New York (2012)
14. Witten, I.H., Frank, E.: Data Mining: Practical Machine Learning Tools and Techniques. Elsevier Inc., Oxford (2005)
15. Watkins, A., Timmis, J., Boggess, L.: Artificial immune recognition system (AIRS): an immune-inspired supervised learning algorithm. Genet. Program. Evolvable Mach. **5**(3), 291–317 (2004)

Link Scheduling for Data Collection in Multichannel Wireless Sensor Networks

Meng-Shiuan Pan$^{(\boxtimes)}$ and Yi-Hsun Lee

Department of Computer Science and Information Engineering,
Tamkang University, 25137 New Taipei City, Taiwan
`mspan@mail.tku.edu.tw`, `601410037@s01.tku.edu.tw`

Abstract. Data collection is a fundamental operation in many wireless sensor network (WSN) applications. Many previous works discuss how to schedule nodes' active and sleep timings to conserve energy and reduce report latency. Recently, some previous works propose to utilize multiple channels to facilitate scheduling. When the network has multiple channels, the report latency can be further reduced since the interferences between transmission pairs can be eliminated. In this work, we consider the network scenarios that there are sufficient channels, and propose a two-phase algorithm. In our algorithm, we first assign slot to transmission pairs and then assign channels to nodes. The assignment sequence is so designed based on some observations on previous works. Simulation results indicate that the proposed scheme can effectively reduce the report latency and the needed numbers channels for multichannel WSNs.

Keywords: Data collection · Graph theory · Multichannel · Scheduling · Wireless sensor network

1 Introduction

Data collection is a fundamental operation in many *wireless sensor network* (*WSN*) applications including monitoring [5,10], health care [6], dynamic path finding [1,11], and smart home [9]. In this scenario, there is a set of nodes periodically report their sensory data via a reporting tree to a sink node. Two technical issues are concerned when gathering data. The first one is how to conserve energy consumption. To conserve energy, many previous works discuss to allow nodes to switch between active and sleep mode. By the setting, a parent and child pair needs to wake up in the assigned *time slots*. During the time slot, the parent node collects data from the child node. In the scenario, a parent node may need to wake up multiple slots if it has more than one child node. The parent node can be configured to aggregate all its child nodes' reports to one report before reporting to its parent. Moreover, the second issue is how to reduce report latency. We can see that in order to conserve report latency, the active timings of all parent and child pairs should be carefully designed.

Figure 1(a) shows an example of slot assignment, where a digit nearby a tree link is the assigned slot for the upward link (to the sink). To reduce report

© Institute for Computer Sciences, Social Informatics and Telecommunications Engineering 2015
J. Jung et al. (Eds.): INFOSCALE 2014, LNICST 139, pp. 80–90, 2015.
DOI: 10.1007/978-3-319-16868-5_8

latency, we can assign a slot to a link with a larger slot number than its descendant links'. However, when deciding slots, some adjacent links cannot use the same slot. For example, in Fig. 1(a), when the pairs (u, v) and (x, y) use the same slot, the receivers v will be interfered by x. In the example, the links $(v, sink)$ and (x, y) cannot use the same slot because that the transmissions of v will interfere with the receptions of y. Moreover, in Fig. 1(a), the reports from node u will have the longest report latency, i.e., u's reports need four slots to arrive the sink.

Recently, the multiple channel concept is discussed to be able to facilitate slot assignment. When the network has multiple channels, each node can be assigned to a frequency channel to communicate with its child nodes. An in-tree node needs to switch between two channels: one for collecting reports from its child nodes and one for reporting data to its parent. For a leaf node, it only needs to stay in its parent's channel. With multiple channels, the interferences between links can be eliminated, and thus can have the benefit of reducing report latency. For example, in Fig. 1(b), when the node y uses channel 1, the link (x, y) can be assigned to slot 1. Although the pairs $(v, sink)$ and (x, y) are assigned to the same slot, the transmissions of v will not interfere with node y (since these two pairs operate on different frequency channels). In Fig. 1(b), the node z will have the longest report latency. Compare to the assignment in Fig. 1(a), the longest report latency can be reduced from four slots to two slots.

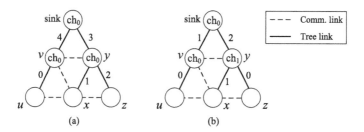

Fig. 1. The network scenario.

In this work, we design a slot and channel assignment scheme for fast data collection in low-powered multiple-channel WSNs. We assume that nodes adopt the IEEE 802.15.4 radio interfaces. In IEEE 802.15.4, there are 27 usable frequency channels [7]. Refer to the references [3,4], we also consider the scenario that the network density is not so high and the network has *sufficient channels* to eliminate interferences between transmission pairs. We propose a slot and channel assignment scheme, which contains two phases: First, the slot assignment phase decides the link schedule based on the given tree topology. The goal of this phase is to minimize the report latency of the network. Second, the channel assignment phase tries to use less numbers of channels to eliminate interferences between links. The simulation results indicate that the proposed scheme can indeed achieve our goal. Moreover, we remark that why we aim to use less number of channel to eliminate interferences. This is because that if we do so, nodes will have more opportunities to operate on channels that are more clear. More specifically, assume that the channel assignment phase needs c channels to eliminate all interferences. After channel assignment, the network manager can find c clearer channels among all available channels in the environment for nodes.

References [3,8] propose energy efficient or low latency data collection schemes for multichannel WSNs. The references [8] propose tree construction, slot assignment, and channel assignment schemes for data collection for WSNs. In the proposed network scenario, the sensor readings can be aggregated when reporting to the sink. The goal is to minimize the number of used slots (defined as *scheduling length* in [8]) of the network. When constructing the network, the proposed scheme connects nodes by a degree-constraint tree. Each in-tree node will be assigned to a channel, which will not be the same as its nearby in-tree nodes. When scheduling slots, each node greedily selects a minimum-numbered slot, and the selected slot will not be the same its sibling nodes. Moreover, reference [3] shows that when a network has unlimited or limited frequencies, the problem of minimizing the scheduling length is NP-complete. Then, the authors in [3] propose approximation algorithms for the networks with unlimited and limited frequency channels, respectively. Based on the above works [3,8], we have the following observations. First, we observe that minimizing the scheduling length does not imply that the report latency is minimized. Second, in order eliminate possible interferences, the above schemes assign channels to nodes before slot assignment. We observe that some in-tree nodes can be assigned to the same channel since their transmission pairs are scheduled to use different time slots. So, in this work, our policy is to assign slots to links first and then assign channels to nodes. Our policy can effectively use less numbers of channels to eliminate interferences.

The rest of this paper is organized as follows. Sections 2 and 3 present the network models and the proposed scheme, respectively. Simulation results are given in Sect. 4. Finally, Sect. 5 concludes this paper.

2   Network Models

Given a network, we model it by a graph $G = (V, E)$, where V contains all nodes and E contains all symmetric communication links between nodes in V. A node in V is designated as the sink t of the network. All nodes in this network are static, and each node has only one radio transceiver. From G, we construct a BFS tree $T = (V, E_T)$, where E_T represents the tree links that span all V and $|E_T| = |V| - 1$. For an edge $e = (u, v)$ in E_T, we say that the e is a *transmission pair* in the network, and the node v is the parent of u, i.e., $v = par(u)$.

We assume there are k available frequency channels, i.e., k channels, which numbered from 0 to $(k - 1)$. Each in-tree node v will be assigned to a channel $ch(v)$, and v uses the channel $ch(v)$ to communicate with its child nodes. Moreover, we assume that there are n slots, which numbered from 0 to $(n - 1)$.

Each node $v \in \{V \setminus t\}$ will be assigned to a slot $s(v)$. The node v communicates with its parent $par(v)$ at the slot $s(v)$ by its parent's channel $ch(par(v))$. We restrict that in a slot time, a node can only be located in one transmission pair. The root t only stays in channel $ch(t)$. An in-tree node $v \in \{V \setminus t\}$ changes between two channels. More specifically, it switches to channel $ch(v)$ and $ch(par(v))$ to receive its child nodes' reports and to report sensory readings to its parent, respectively. Note that according to the Brook's theorem [12], which proves that m colors are sufficient to color any graph with a maximum degree of m, we would assume that $n \geq D$, where D is the degree of the network.

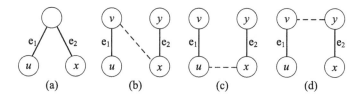

Fig. 2. Interference relationships.

When assigning channels and slots, the interferences between transmission pairs should be avoided. Given the tree $T \in G$, there are two kinds of interferences, say *primary interference* and *indirect interference*. We define two transmission pairs are primary interference if they have a common endpoint in T. Figure 2(a) shows an example that e_1 and e_2 are primary interference. Then, a transmission pair (u, v) is an indirect interference of another transmission pair (x, y) if the transmissions of node u or v cause interference on the receiver of node x or y. Figure 2(b)–(d) shows examples, where we assume all nodes operate on the same channel and the nodes v and y are the parent nodes of u and x, respectively. In these three examples, edges $e_1 = (u, v)$ and $e_2 = (x, y)$ are indirect interferences because of the following reasons. (i) In Fig. 2(b), x's report packets will interfere with the packet receptions of v. (ii) In Fig. 2(c), x's report packets will interfere with the ACK packets receptions of u and vice versa. (iii) In Fig. 2(d), y's ACK packets will interfere with the packet receptions of v and vice versa. When the network has only one channel, two interference transmission pairs cannot be assigned to the same slot. However, when the network has multiple channels, indirect interferences relationship can be eliminated by channel assignments. For example, in Fig. 2(b)(c)(d), edges e_1 and e_2 can use the same slot if nodes v and y are assigned to different channels. By the above discussions, we say that a channel and slot assignment for the network G is *interference-free* if any two transmission pairs, $(u, v) \in E_T$ and $(x, y) \in E_T$, will not interfere with each other.

Given a channel and slot assignment for G based on a tree T, we define the one-hop report latencies of nodes by the following two cases. First, a node $v \in child(t)$, the one-hop report latency of v is zero. Second, a node $v \notin child(t)$, the one-hop report latency of v to its parent $par(v)$ is $(s(par(v)) - s(v)) \mod n$.

Then, we define the report latency $L(v)$ for a node v to the sink t as the sum of one-hop report latencies on the reporting path from v to the sink. The *report latency* $L(G)$ of G is defined as the maximum report latency among all node in V. The *report latency* $L(G)$ of the network G is $\max_{\forall v \in V}\{L(v)\}$.

In this paper, we assume that the network has *sufficient channels*. For a transmission pair (u, v), there are at most $2 \times D$ neighbors nearby u and v. When the number of channels $k \geq (2 \times D)$, we can say that the network has sufficient channels. Then, we can assign different channels to those receivers nearby a transmission pair (u, v).

The problem description of this paper is as follows: *Given a graph $G = (V, E)$, the tree $T \in G$, n available slots, and k available channels, where $k \geq (2 \times D)$, if there exists an interference-free channel and slot assignment such that (1) the $L(G)$ is minimized and (2) the used number of channels is minimized.* In [4], the authors present a similar problem as ours, and the presented problem in [4] is proved as a NP-complete problem. In this work, we propose a heuristic scheme, which is composed of a slot assignment phase and a channel assignment phase as described in the next section.

3   The Proposed Scheme

3.1   The Slot Assignment Phase

Based on T, our goal of slot assignment is to minimize the report latency $L(G)$. In this phase, we assign slots to nodes in T by a top-down manner. We first assign the sink t's slot $s(t)$ to be $n - 1$, and then we execute the following steps.

1. Based on T, we decide a sequence S of slot assignment by traversing nodes from t in a level-by-level fashion. In a level, we sort nodes in that level by their numbers of descendant nodes in descending order. Then, we check the next level until the sequence S is decided.
2. When S is not empty, we extract the first node, say v, from S. For v, we assign a slot $s(v)$ to it, which can satisfy the following two conditions:
   - The $s(v)$ can result in the least one-hop report latency to $par(v)$.
   - The $s(v)$ does not induce primary interferences.

Note that, in step 1, the node with more descendant nodes will have a higher priority. This design is to increase the probability that the descendant nodes that are located in a larger subtree can report their data earlier. When assigning slot to a node v in step 2, we only consider v's primary interferences. After the slot assignment, indirect interferences can further be removed in the channel assignment phase.

3.2   The Channel Assignment Phase

In this phase, we aim to use the least number of channels to remove indirect interferences. Without loss of generality, we first assume that all nodes' default channels are channel numbered 0. Refer to Fig. 2, we can find that for a node v, (1) the corresponding tree links of v's child nodes' neighbors, say $N^T(C(v))$, and (2) the corresponding tree links of v's not-in-tree neighbors, say $N^T(N(v))$, may cause interference with transmissions or receptions of v. In the following, we define an in-tree node v's *interference neighbor pairs*, which cause interferences with the transmission between v and its child nodes.

Definition 1. *Given the slot assignment in G and the channel c, a pair $(x, par(x))$ is one of the* interference neighbor pairs *of an in-tree node v based on channel c, say $I(v, c)$, if the following three conditions are satisfied. (C1) both x and $par(x)$ belong to $\{N^T(C(v)) \cup N^T(N(v))\}$. (C2) $ch(par(x)) = ch(v) = c$. (C3) $s(x)$ is the same as $s(v)$ or any $s(u)$, where $u \in child(v)$.*

The conditions C2 and C3 are to restrict that the pair $(x, par(x))$ operates in the same channel of v and the used slot is the same as one of v's child node, respectively. Figure 3 shows an example that before channel assignment, the $I(u, 0)$ contains the pairs $(x, par(x))$ and $(y, par(u))$. So, given a tree T, the slot assignment, and k channels, the channel assignment procedures work as follows.

1. For all in-tree nodes, we sort them according to their priorities, where a node v is considered to have a higher priority than u if one of the following condition is satisfied: (i) $|I(v, 0)| > |I(u, 0)|$. (ii) $|I(v, 0)| = |I(u, 0)|$ and $ID(v) > ID(u)$. After sorting, we put those in-tree nodes into a list S.
2. When S is not empty, we extract the first node, say v, from S, and decide $ch(v)$. We set a variable $c = 0$. Then, we check if $I(v, c) = \emptyset$. If so, we can set $ch(v) = c$, and finish the channel assignment of v. Otherwise, we set $c = c + 1$ and then execute this step again.

Note that in step 1, a node v with a larger $I(v, 0)$ should assign to a channel earlier because that it has less choice of channels. In step 2, we greedily find a channel that the node v can use.

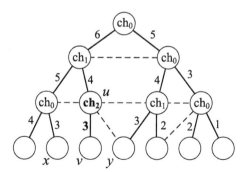

Fig. 3. An example of the observation on channel assignment.

After assigning slots and channels, we observe that the used number of channels can further be reduced if we can modify some link's slots. For example, in the slot and channel assignment result in Fig. 3, node u is assigned to ch_2 to avoid interfering with the transmission pairs $(x, par(x))$ and $(y, par(y))$. From the result, the network needs three channels to eliminate all indirect interferences, and the report latency $L(G) = 5$. From Fig. 3, we can see that if we "loosen" the slot of node v from $s(v) = 3$ to $s(v) = 2$, the node u can change to use the ch_0. After the modification, the $I(u, 0) = \emptyset$ and the $L(G)$ is unchanged. But, the needed numbers of channels will be reduced from three to two.

By the above observation, in this work, we further propose a *channel adjustment algorithm*, which works as follows. For those in-tree nodes, we sort them according to their assigned channel numbers in a non-increasing order. After sorting, we put them into a list S. When S is not empty, we extract the first node, say u, from S. For each node u, we set a variable $c' = 0$ and then perform the following steps.

1. We check if $c' = ch(u)$. If so, the channel of u cannot be modified, and the procedure ends. Otherwise, we put those transmission pairs in $I(u, c')$ into a queue Q.
2. If Q is empty, we can go to step 3. Otherwise, we set $(x, par(x)) = dequeue(Q)$, and perform the following checks.
   (a) If $s(x)$ is *not* the same as the slots of u and u's child nodes, the pair $(x, par(x))$ will not interfere with $(u, par(u))$. In this case, we re-perform the step 2 to check the next transmission pair in Q.
   (b) If $s(x)$ is the same as the slot of u or any of u's in-tree child nodes, the pair $(x, par(x))$ interferes with $(u, par(u))$. In this case, the channel c' cannot be used by u. So, we set $c' = c' + 1$ and go back to step 1.
   (c) If $s(x)$ is the same as the slot of a u's leaf child node, say v, we can try to modify the $s(v)$ by the following steps.
      i. We set $s_{tmp}(v) = s(v)$.
      ii. We greedily modify $s_{tmp}(v) = (s_{tmp}(v) - 1) \bmod n$, and then test if (i) $I(u, c') = \emptyset$ and (ii) $L(G)$ is preserved when we pretend node v adopts the slot $s_{tmp}(v)$.
      iii. If a $s_{tmp}(v)$ is found, we record the $s_{tmp}(v)$ for v and re-perform the step 2. Otherwise, the c' cannot be used by u, and then we set $c' = c' + 1$ and go back to step 1.
3. In this step, we can set $ch(u) = c'$, and modify the slot of u's leaf child nodes (that has demanded to change slots in step 2.c.iii) to their new slots.

Note that in the above procedure, we only try to modify the slots of leaf nodes, and do not modify the slots of in-tree nodes. This is because that if changing an in-tree nodes slots, we may need to modify the slots of corresponding ancestor or descendant nodes' slots, and computational complexity will be high. Also note that when performing the procedure in step 2.c.iii, we guarantee that the network can still be interference-free and $L(G)$ can be preserved.

3.3   Time Complexity Analysis

The computational complexity of this algorithm is analyzed as follows. First, in the step 1 of slot assignment phase, it takes $O(|V|log(|V|))$ time to sort nodes.

In the step 2, when deciding a slot, each node needs to check at most $O(D^2)$ transmission pairs nearby it. So, the complexity of step 2 is $O(|V|D^2)$. The complexity of the slot assignment phase will be dominated by $O(|V|D^2)$. Second, before the sorting procedure in step 1 of the channel assignment, each node, say v, needs to calculate $I(v, 0)$, and the cost of deriving nodes' interference neighbors will be $O(|V|D^2)$. The sorting procedure also costs $O(|V|log(|V|))$ time. In the step 2, for a node v, we need to traverse $O(D^2)$ neighbors to decide whether v can use a channel numbered c. Since there are k channels and $|V|$ nodes, the complexity of step 2 will be $O(k|V|D^2)$. As a result, the complexity of the channel assignment will be $O(k|V|D^2)$. Third, we analyze the channel adjustment algorithm in the channel assignment phase. In the step 1, we need $O(|V|log(|V|))$ time to sort nodes. In the step 2, a node will test at most k channels, and there are at most $O(D^2)$ transmission pairs in Q. For a transmission pair, we have to perform at most D checks. So, the complexity of step 2 will be $O(|V| \times k \times D^2 \times D) = O(k|V|D^3)$, which dominates the complexity of the channel adjustment algorithm. To summarize, the overall complexity will be dominated by the channel adjustment procedure, and the computational complexity of the proposed scheme is $O(k|V|D^3)$.

4   Simulation Results

In this work, we develop a simulator (by C programming language) to verify the proposed scheme. We compare the proposed scheme (denoted by SF) against the proposed scheme in [3] (denoted by CF) and a greedy top-down slot and channel assignment scheme (denoted by TD) [2]. In TD, the authors assign slot and channel to nodes at the same time. For a node, the TD greedily selects a slot and a channel, which can minimize the node's one hop latency and eliminate interferences between the node and its neighbors, respectively. In our simulations, we further show the results of the reduced version of SF (denoted by rSF), which does not perform channel adjustment procedures. We compare the network latency $L(G)$ (in unit of slots) and the number of used channels.

We first simulate the networks with size ranged from 100^2 m^2 to 190^2 m^2, and we generate $100^2/100$ to $190^2/100$ nodes randomly distributed in the network. The transmission ranges of nodes are fixed to 25 m. Figure 4(a) shows the results of $L(G)$. In this simulation, when the network size becomes larger, the results on $L(G)$ are expected to become longer. We can see that the SF and rSF can outperform the other two schemes in $L(G)$, and the performances of SF and rSF are almost the same. In Fig. 4(b), we can see that TD uses the least number of channels. However, as shown in Fig. 4(a), the TD will induce the longest $L(G)$. This result indicates that when selecting slot and channels at the same time, the available channels cannot be fully utilized. According to Fig. 4(b), the SF needs less numbers of channels than rSF, which demonstrates the effectiveness of the channel adjustment algorithm. From Fig. 4(a) and (b), the SF outperforms the CF in both $L(G)$ and the numbers of used channels. This result demonstrates that our policy (which assigns slot and then assigns channels) is better than the one (which assigns channels and then assigns slots) used by the CF.

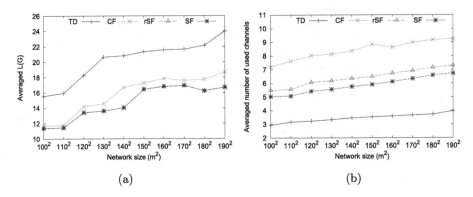

Fig. 4. Simulation results of (a) averaged $L(G)$ and (b) averaged used number of channels with varied network size.

Next, we simulate the network with size fixed to be $100^2 \, \mathrm{m}^2$, and the network contains 100 nodes. We vary the transmission ranges of nodes from 17 m to 26 m. The results are shown in Fig. 5. In Fig. 5(a), when the transmission ranges of nodes are 19 m, the $L(G)$ values of these four schemes are lower. This is because that the longest hop count distance to the sink decreases. When the transmission range becomes larger ($\geq 20 \, \mathrm{m}$), nodes will have more interference neighbors, and thus the $L(G)$ may become longer. We can see that the SF can still outperform other three schemes in $L(G)$. Again, in the Fig. 5(b), the SF consumes more numbers of channels than TD, but the SF induces less $L(G)$.

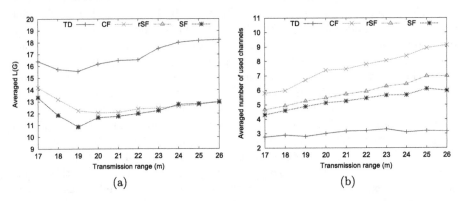

Fig. 5. Simulation results of (a) averaged $L(G)$ and (b) averaged used number of channels with varied transmission ranges.

5 Conclusions

In this work, we propose a slot and channel assignment scheme for data collection in multiple channel WSNs. We assume that the network has sufficient frequency channels. We design a two phase algorithm to assign slots and channels to nodes. In the slot assignment phase, we aim to schedule slots for transmission pairs to reduce the report latency. Then, in the channel assignment phase, we aim to eliminate indirect interferences with less channels. To reduce the needed number of channels, our scheme may reassign some links' slots, and then to adjust the channel assignments. Our scheme can eliminate interferences by less channels, and thus nodes can operate on channels that are more clear. Simulation results indicate that the propose scheme can indeed achieve low latency data collection by less frequency channels. In the future, it is deserved to consider that the scenario that network has limited amount of channels.

Acknowledgments. M.-S. Pan's research is sponsored by NSC grant 103-2221-E-032-030.

References

1. Chen, P.-Y., Chen, W.-T., Tseng, Y.-C., Huang, C.-F.: Providing group tour guide by RFIDs and wireless sensor networks. IEEE Trans. Wirel. Commun. **8**(6), 3059–3067 (2009)
2. Ghods, F., Yousefi, H., Afshin Hemmatyar, A.M., Movaghar, A.: MC-MLAS: multi-channel minimum latency aggregation scheduling in wireless sensor networks. Elsevier Comput. Netw. **57**(18), 3812–3825 (2013)
3. Ghosh, A., Incel, Ö.D., Kumar, V., Krishnamachari, B.: Multichannel scheduling and spanning trees: throughput-delay tradeoff for fast data collection in sensor networks. IEEE/ACM Trans. Netw. **19**(6), 1731–1744 (2011)
4. Ghosh, A., Incel, Ö.D., Kumar, V.A., Krishnamachari, B.: Multi-channel scheduling algorithms for fast aggregated convergecast in sensor networks. In: Proceedings of IEEE Mobile Adhoc and Sensor Systems Conference (MASS) (2009)
5. Hayes, J., Beirne, S., Lau, K.-T., Diamond, D.: Evaluation of a low cost wireless chemical sensor network for environmental monitoring. In: Proceedings of IEEE Sensors Conference (2008)
6. Huo, H., Xu, Y., Zhang, H., Chuang, Y.-H., Wu, T.-C.: Wireless-sensor-networks-based healthcare system: a survey on the view of communication paradigms. Int. J. Ad Hoc Ubiquit. Comput. (IJAHUC) **8**(3), 135–154 (2011)
7. IEEE standard for information technology - telecommunications and information exchange between systems - local and metropolitan area networks specific requirements part 15.4: wireless medium access control (MAC) and physical layer (PHY) specifications for low-rate wireless personal area networks (LR-WPANs) (revision of IEEE Std 802.15.4-2003) (2006)
8. Incel, Ö.D., Krishnamachari, B.: Enhancing the data collection rate of tree-based aggregation in wireless sensor networks. In: Proceedings of IEEE Sensor and Ad Hoc Communications and Networks Conference (SECON) (2008)
9. Nguyen, N.-H., Tran, Q.-T., Leger, J.-M., Vuong, T.-P.: A real-time control using wireless sensor network for intelligent energy management system in buildings. In: Proceedings of IEEE Workshop on Environmental Energy and Structural Monitoring Systems (EESMS) (2010)
10. Pan, M.-S., Tseng, Y.-C.: Zigbee-based long-thin wireless sensor networks: address assignment and routing schemes. Int. J. Ad Hoc Ubiquit. Comput. (IJAHUC) **12**(3), 147–156 (2013)

11. Tseng, Y.-C., Pan, M.-S., Tsai, Y.-Y.: Wireless sensor networks for emergency navigation. IEEE Comput. **39**(7), 55–62 (2006)
12. West, D.B.: Introduction to Graph Theory. Prentice Hall, USA (2001)

A Design of Sensor Data Ontology for a Large Scale Crop Growth Environment System

Eunji Lee[✉], Byeongkyu Ko, Chang Choi, and Pankoo Kim

Department of Computer Engineering, Chosun University, 309 Pilmun-Daero,
Donggu, Gwangju, Republic of Korea
{eunbesu,byeonkyu.ko,enduranceaura}@gmail.com,
pkkim@chosun.ac.kr

Abstract. The development of various sensor and sensor network made it possible to collect environmental date from specific area, however, there is a lack of practical application to share useful information and knowledge with using the sensor data, Thus this study is to establish data domain ontology and to predict the information on the growth environment of crop based on this already built domain ontology. The inference model suggested in this paper is collected from weather center.

1 Introduction

Recently the natural condition and ecosystem has faced with rapid change as the environmental pollution and the climate change became more serious. The importance of continuous study on environment and ecosystem became a big concern under the inexperience change of environmental condition [1]. For the local industry, especially, environmental condition affects greatly on yields, active risk management system that combines diverse information on climate, weather, cultivation situation is urgent. Thus, there is a need to collect and analyze the observation data by long-term and national level of monitoring on environment to upgrade the accuracy of prediction on environmental change. The environmental sensor network can be used for the environmental monitoring. The advanced IT technology made this monitoring effective with the environmental sensor data by checking all details in minutes and in wide area. Despite there have been active ongoing studies on collection, repository and process of sensor stream data to establish environmental monitoring system so far, the development of application such as predicating model on the growth environment of crop is relatively insufficient. Therefore, this study is to establish data domain ontology for analyzing intelligent sensor data and to build up inference model to predict the information on the growth environment of crop based on this already built domain ontology for increasing productivity, efficiency and quality of crops.

2 Related Work

2.1 Environmental Sensor Networks

The sensor network is a overall system [2] to collect, control and analyze outlook information anytime by distributing multiple light sensor node in any spaces and areas

© Institute for Computer Sciences, Social Informatics and Telecommunications Engineering 2015
J. Jung et al. (Eds.): INFOSCALE 2014, LNICST 139, pp. 91–96, 2015.
DOI: 10.1007/978-3-319-16868-5_9

needed to be monitored. It can be applied to any things and environment where can be monitored by attaching sensors for real time monitoring and management such as animal management, patient management, home network, environmental pollution monitoring and toll gates [3]. Thus, environmental sensor network is a word refers to one of general words for monitoring environment, eco-temperature, humidity, insolation and velocity. The study on existing environmental sensor networks are the one for designing the sensor data management system to support monitoring system of sensor data that can deal with query collected from DBMS [4]. Another one is for establishing sensor network ontology that shares data and concerns recycle to support efficient intelligent service from real time stream data [5].

2.2 Ontology Based Sensor Networks

Ontology is defined by conceptualization specification to help human and program to share the knowledge on a specific domain [6]. There are three advantages in ontology. First, the sharing of knowledge. Using ontology make it easy to assemble general concept on domain while the different agent and service are interacting under the semantic web and ubiquitous circumstance. Second, the reusing of knowledge and information. It makes it easier to compose ontology by reusing different domain or other well- defined domain. OWL(Web Ontology Language, the latest word suggested by W3C(World Wide Web Consortium) is widely used for building ontology. It is recognized to have better quality in expression by adding a vocabulary with formal semantic. Third, enabling logic inference. As the ontology can be expressed based on description logic of human knowledge, it can make diverse logic inference mechanism [7, 8]. In this respect, the sensor ontology can design the sensor ontology applying for sensor space to build ontology by retrieving words to express the meaning of data and define the relation of the words. The sensor network based on ontology, especially, has the limelight as it can collect and share not only the information of traffic condition and location but also other various information. It is also popular for it can be connected with existing internet or web based system [5]. This paper suggests the studies to solve the problems of meaning difference between sensor network and to infer the information on crop growth environment by applying ontology between different sensor environment data. It extracts words and define the relation between words to explain the meaning of date collected form sensor to difference sensor network applying ontology to different environment sensors based on relation of diverse sensor data.

3 A Design of Sensor Data Ontology

3.1 Architecture of Crop Growth Environment System

This paper describes an ontology for describing data collected from sensor networks for crop growth environment inference. By applying the rules and statistical method based on the relationships among the various sensor data, it is possible to infer the growth environment of the crop. Figure 1 is an overall system architecture of the proposed sensor data ontology.

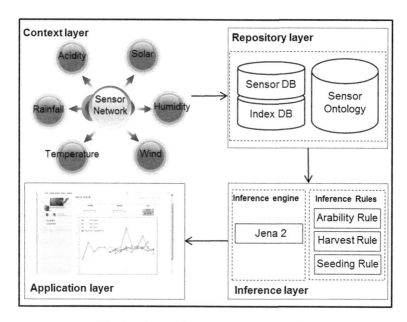

Fig. 1. The Architecture of proposed system

The 'Context Layer' is a module used to collect context information from sensors, Context information consist of various sensor data such as solar, wind, acidity, temperature, humidity. Identified context information generates event from context generating module in the context layer. Context Instance Generation generates query to infer ontology and converts into OWL which is a readable form by ontology. Converted OWL data is sent to Repository Layer. In the 'Inference Layer', the transmitted information is converted into queries to be inferred to the ontology and the users' health state will then be inferred. For the inference, the 'Inference Rule' defined by the 'Crop Ontology' and by the professional specialist(s) will be referred. After completing the service inference, the type of service to be provided to users can use such services through the 'Application Layer'.

3.2   Establishment of Sensor Data Ontology

Collected sensor data builds database. The upper ontology of crops built for control intelligent sensor data which is keeping the sensor database is proper for sharing and reuse and it is able to reduce the time for development and resource. For this work, selecting domain based on DB and setting sub class should come first. Then design the general structure of domain ontology to present information used withing the sensor data analysis system. The definitions of concept necessary for sensor ontology construction are as following Table 1.

'Product' is the highest class that has Descriptor class which describes Domain class and sensor data as its lower class. Context class is built to retrieve information of the places and time of the data by describing the property of sensor data in detail.

Table 1. The Composition of Conceptual Ontology

Class			Specification
Domain			- Classification for crops - Used for classification of data of cops
Description	Identifier		- The Serial number of sensor - DB Key replacing title
	Data Type		- The types of sensor data - Classifying properties on temperature, humidity, velocity, wind direction
	Keyword		- Index Keyword
	Writer		- Information holder
	Context	Location	- Local information
		Spatio	- Space information
		Temporal	- Time

The property of object is for describing the relation of classes. The object properties defined by OWL ontology of this development system are shown as in Table 2. Restriction is supposed to specify the condition for an element to be a component of class. Connecting between properties information of classes and domains selected to build ontology is necessary and Table 3 is an example of the property information by specific task.

Table 2. Identification of Object Property

Object property	Domain	Range	Restriction	Represent
hasDomain	Identifier	Domain	Min 1	Identifier class owns over two components of domain class
hasKeyword	Identifier	Keyword	Some	Identifier class owns the components of Keyword class its components
hasWriter	Identifier	Writer	Some	Identifier class owns the components of writer as its components
hasLoaction	Identifier	Location	Exactly 1	Identifier class owns the components of location as its components
hasDataType	Identifier	DataType	Some	Identifier class owns the components of Datatype class its components
hasSpatio	Location	Spatio	Some	Location class owns the components of Spatio class its components

Table 3. An Example of the Property Information

<name of crops rdf:ID="ProductSystem">
<ProductType rdf:resource="**#corn**" />
<ProccessType rdf:resource="**#Harvest**" />
<hasSalinity rdf:datatype="&xsd;string">300</hasLocation>
<hasRainfall rdf:datatype="&xsd;string">500</hasLocation>

4   A Design of Inference Rules Using Sensor Data Ontology

Retrieval method of semantic retrieval system is to refining whole resource applying inference and respond to the query of users using semantic inference retrieval engine. This semantic retrieval system apprehends the users' intention and draws out the result that is impossible by general keyword matching to substantial expansion of retrieval domain. Temperature adaptability, rainfall, soil acidity are selected as the properties of determinant of yield based on information of crop cultivation environment. The Table 4 is an example of inference rule with yield determinant basis sampling cultivation environment of corn.

Table 4. Design of Inference Rules based on Description Logic

//Predicate declarations
hasTemperature(Month,Temperature) *hasRainfall(Monath,Rainfall)* *has Acidity(x_n, Acidity)*
Month = {Jan, Feb, Mar, Apr, ... , Nov, Dec}
//Rules
∀Location = $x_1,x_2,$ ... ,x_n
hasAcidity(x_n, Acidity) ∧ 5. 5 ≤ Acidity ≤ 8.0 ⇒ SuitableLocation(x_n)
hasTemperature(Month,Temperature)∧hasRainfall(Month,Rainfall)⇒SuitableLocation(x_n)

From the collected data, the inference rule predicts the result applying crop ontology that has the properties of yield determinant of temperature adaptability, rainfall, soil acidity. Then the cultivation suitability can be inferred by inference rule and the area suits for crop cultivation is to selected from the result of inference (Table 5).

Table 5. The Example of Ontology Inference results

July	Temperature	Rainfall	Acidity	Cultivation suitability (%)
A location	36 °C	80 mm	pH 9.0	82 %
B location	32 °C	120 mm	pH 5.5	90 %

5 Conclusion

Development of divers sensor is on going as the importance of sensor network is on the rise. Consequently, it is now possible to collect various environmental information. This paper is a study to provide service for predicting crop growth environment by analyzing environment sensor date. It is to establish sensor data ontology collected from sensor network and apply inference rules based on condition for crop growth environment to predict the time of harvest. seeding and cultivation suitability. The inference model suggested on this paper operated simulation with data collected form weather center. It will be able to increase efficiency, productivity and quality of crop by applying this study to crop growth environment.

Acknowledgments. This work (Grants No. C0250284) was supported by Business for Cooperative R&D between Industry, Academy, and Research Institute funded Korea Small and Medium Business Administration in 2014 and This research was supported by Basic Science Research Program through the National Research Foundation of Korea (NRF) funded by the Ministry of Education (No. 2013R1A1A2A10011667).

References

1. Tubaishat, M., Madria, S.: Sensor networks: an overview. IEEE Potentials **22**(2), 20–23 (2003)
2. Busang, C., Wuchul, J., Jeongtak, R., Yeonbo, K.: A design of room temperature measurement system on wireless environment. J. Comput. Commun. Res. **3**(2), 45–50 (2004)
3. Daniel, J.A., Wolfgan, L., Samuel, M., Jörg, S.: An integration framework for sensor networks and data stream management systems. In: Proceedings of the International Conference on Very Large Data Bases, vol. 30, pp. 1361–1364 (2004)
4. Jason, J.J.: Ontology based preprocessing scheme for mining data streams from sensor networks. J. Intell. Inf. Syst. **5**(3), 67–80 (2009)
5. Chang, C., Junho, C., Pankoo, K.: Ontology-based access control model for security policy reasoning in cloud computing. J. Supercomput. **67**(3), 711–722 (2014). (Springer Science +Business Media New York)
6. Ian, H., Peter F.P., Harold, B., Said, T., Benjamin, G., Mike, D.: SWRL: A Semantic Web Rule Language Combining OWL and RuleML. W3C member submission (2004). http://www.w3.org/Submission/SWRL/
7. Ian, H., Lei, L., Daniele, T.: The instance store: description logic reasoning with large numbers of individuals. In: International Workshop on Description Logics, pp. 31–40 (2004)
8. Chang, C., Miyoung, C., Myunggwon, H.: Travel ontology for intelligent recommendation system. In: Third Asia International Conference on Modelling and Simulation, pp. 637–642. IEEE (2009)

Real-Time Data Flow Language Processing System for Handling Streams of Data

Choon Seo Park(✉), Jin-Hwan Jeong, Myungcheol Lee, Yong-Ju Lee,
Miyoung Lee, and Sung Jin Hur

Bigdata Platform Research Department, Electronics and Telecommunication
Research Institute (ETRI), 161, Gajeong-Dong, Yuseong-Gu, Daejeon, Korea
{parkcs,jhjeong,mclee,yongju,mylee,sjheo}@etri.re.kr

Abstract. Apache Pig system generates MapReduce jobs by compiling program scripts written in Pig Latin to process large data sets in parallel on distributed computing nodes. There are inefficient features in Pig due to the limitation of the MapReduce, e.g., the MapReduce is used only for batch processing. As various smart devices are extensively utilized recently, streams of data are generated explosively and the need to process streams of data in real-time is required. In this paper, we propose a data flow language processing system, called LAMA-CEP, by generating DAG-based stream processing services to process unbounded streams of data in real-time continuously. We present a stream processing language, called Pig Latin Stream extended from Pig Latin. Programs written in Pig Latin Stream are translated into distributed stream processing jobs and then the jobs are executed on a highly scalable distributed stream processing system to process large streams of data in real-time.

Keywords: Data flow language · Real-time processing · Distributed data stream processing

1 Introduction

As data sets have explosively increased, there have been proposed big data platforms for processing huge data sets. Hadoop MapReduce platform is a representative data processing scheme for handling large data sets on distributed computing nodes [1–3]. The Hadoop platform can support highly scalable distributed data processing capabilities, but it is difficult to program and easy to make serious errors because it supports a low-level interface. In order to solve these problems, the apache Pig platform has been proposed [4, 5]. The apache Pig system provides a high-level interface language, called Pig Latin. Pig system enables users to generate data processing services with ease of development, high productivity by using a high-level data flow Pig Latin language. Pig system compiles Pig Latin programs, which are abstract data flow expressions, into one or more physical data flow jobs, and then orchestrates the execution of these jobs. And the complied service jobs are executed on the MapReduce engine. The MapReduce platform is suitable for batch processing on large data sets. As smart devices like various sensors, smart phones, smart TV, and so on are emerging extensively in recent years, streams of data are consistently generated exponentially [6]

© Institute for Computer Sciences, Social Informatics and Telecommunications Engineering 2015
J. Jung et al. (Eds.): INFOSCALE 2014, LNICST 139, pp. 97–106, 2015.
DOI: 10.1007/978-3-319-16868-5_10

and the data processing platforms are required to handle and analyze the large unbounded streams of data in real-time. However, the existing MapReduce platform, batch processing engine, cannot support to process unbounded streams of data in real-time. To handle huge continuous streams of data, new stream processing schemes have been proposed, e.g. Storm [7] and S4 [8]. Storm and S4 can process unbounded streams of data in real-time. However, the users have difficulty for programming skills on Storm and S4 because they only provide distributed stream models. Therefore, the mechanisms that can process streams of data in real-time with providing a high-level interface language like Pig Latin are required. Therefore, we propose a data flow language processing platform for processing unbounded streams of data with a data flow language. The proposed processing platform has been developed, based on Pig system. To support data stream processing in real-time, the generated stream processing service jobs in our platform are executed not on the MapReduce engine but on distributed stream processing platform, self-developed system.

The rest of the paper is organized as follows. In the next section, we introduce the overview of Pig system, and existing distributed stream processing platforms. In Sect. 3, we present real-time data flow language processing system to process unbounded streams of data. In Sect. 4, we describe the current implementation techniques of proposed data flow language processing system. Finally, we conclude our work in Sect. 5.

2   Related Works

In this section, we briefly describe the overview and some drawbacks of Apache Pig system. We also address existing distributed stream processing systems.

2.1   Apache Pig

Apache Pig is an open-source platform for analyzing enormous data sets that consists of a high-level language for expressing data analysis programs, coupled with infra-structure for evaluating these programs. It supports the parallel programming model of MapReduce jobs to be executed on a Hadoop cluster system. The infrastructure layer of apache Pig is composed of a compiler that generates sequences of MapReduce programs, for which large-scale parallel implementations already exist. The language layer in Pig system currently consists of a simple scripting language, called Pig Latin. The Pig Latin is a procedural language that explicitly defines the data flow, so we can easily create the program for data processing. It supports optimization opportunities, so users can focus on semantics rather than efficiency. Also, users can create their own functions, user-defined functions (UDFs), to do special-purpose processing. Pig supports basic relational operators for processing large data sets. The basic operators of Pig are listed in Table 1. Figure 1 shows the compilation of Pig Latin and execution processing of a translated stream service in Pig. Apache Pig takes Pig Latin scripts as an input source. Next, the Pig Latin programs will be compiled as one or more Map-Reduce jobs. There are several stages of compilation such as parsing, semantic checking, optimizations, and translators. Next, a translated MapReduce jobs jar is launched on

Hadoop cluster of computers. Finally the MapReduce jobs are executed on a given Hadoop cluster systems.

Because Pig Latin scripts are translates to a set of MapReduce jobs, the scheduling mechanism of MapReduce jobs is needed. Also, intermediate data files are saved to transmit data among MapReduce jobs, Pig system cannot directly is applied on real-time streams of data processing system.

Table 1. Basic operators of Pig system.

Operators	Definition
Load	Read data from file system
Store	Write data to file system
Foreach	Apply expression to each record and output one or more records
Group/cogroup	Apply predicate and remove records that do not return true
Join	Collect records with the same key form one or more inputs
Order by	Sorts a relation based on one or more fields
Distinct	Remove duplicate records
Union	Merge tow data sets
Split	Split data into 2 or more sets, based on filter conditions
Stream	Send all records through a user provided executable
Sample	Read a random sample of the data
Limit	Limit the number of records

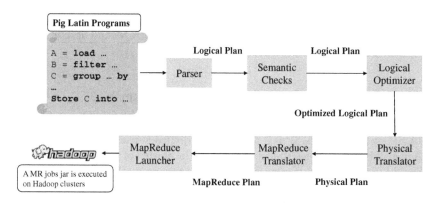

Fig. 1. The process of compilation for Pig Latin programs.

2.2 Existing Distributed Stream Data Processing Systems

Hadoop MapReduce is a batch-processing system for parallel processing of large data sets on cluster system. So, Hadoop MapReduce cannot handle unbounded streams of data. To process huge streams of data in real-time, distributed stream processing mechanisms have been developed. There are two representative distributed data processing systems such as Storm and S4.

Apache Storm is a free and open source distributed real-time computation system for processing fast, large streams of data on a cluster of computers. Storm makes it easy to reliably process unbounded streams of data, doing for real-time processing what Hadoop did for batch processing. Spouts and bolts in Storm are connected with a directed acyclic graph (DAG) and are executed as many tasks across the cluster system. Storm may be used in many fields: real-time analytics, online machine learning, continuous computation, ETL, and more.

S4 (Simple Scalable Streaming System) is a general-purpose, distributed, scalable, fault-tolerant, pluggable platform that allows programmers to easily develop applications for processing continuous, unbounded streams of data.

3   Real-Time Dataflow Language Processing System

Apache Pig system creates MapReduce service job for processing huge data sets on Hadoop cluster system. The MapReduce cannot process unbounded streams of data, consistently generated exponentially. Therefore, we propose a data flow language processing platform, called LAMA-CEP, for processing unbounded streams of data. LAMA-CEP is based on Pig system to use a data flow langue, Pig Latin. Because Pig system is originally designed for batch processing, to process streams of data continuously, LAMA-CEP has been extended from Pig system. We present a stream processing language, called Pig Latin Stream extended from Pig Latin. LAMA-CEP takes a script written in Pig Latin Stream language and translates it into distributed stream processing service, to be executed on distributed stream processing platform, called LAMA-SP like Apache Storm. LAMA-SP is system for processing large streams of data. LAMA-CEP also provides window operators to process unbounded stream data.

In this paper, we briefly introduce the concept of LAMA-SP and describe LAMA-CEP system in detail.

3.1   Distributed Stream Processing Platform (LAMA-SP)

We have developed a distributed stream processing platform like Storm and S4, called LAMA-SP system. LAMA-SP is a real-time distributed stream processing system for processing unbounded large streams of data on a cluster of computers. LAMA-SP supports a DAG-based programing model and processing mechanisms for unbounded input stream of data with key/value data model. The salient property of LAMA-SP is that it supports distributed and parallel processing mechanisms for large streams of data and also supports failover module for crashes of systems.

3.2   Architecture of LAMA-CEP

Because LAMA-CEP is based on Pig system, the architecture of LAMA-CEP is similar to that of Pig system as shown in Fig. 2. Basic components in LAMA-CEP such as a parser and basic operators are close to properties of Pig system. There are largely changed components such as modules for the creation and execution of distributed stream processing service and Input/Output (IO) modules for tuple stream for creating distributed stream processing service jobs to be executed on LAMA-SP distributed stream processing system. Because Pig system originally is designed for supporting MapReduce jobs for batch processing on data files, Pig system only provides file IO functions. To deal incoming streams of data through network, the IO modules of LAMA-CEP have been extended to support network-based IO functions such as TCP and UDP network communications. Window functions have been added in IO modules to handle unbounded stream of data. Existing Pig system creates MapReduce jobs for batch processing. On the other hand, the service creation modules in LAMA-CEP generates DAG-based distributed stream processing service jobs jar with LAMA-SP interface for query processing over data streams continuously. The service execution modules submit the stream processing service jobs generated by the service creation modules to LAMA-SP engine and the submitted stream processing service jobs are executed on LAMA-SP cluster systems.

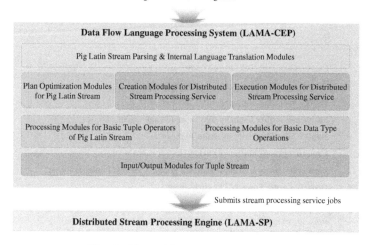

Fig. 2. The architecture of LAMA-CEP

3.3   Pig Latin Stream

Existing Pig Latin supports only batch processing because Pig system is originally designed for Hadoop MapReduce. That is to say, the Pig Latin cannot support to handle unbounded streams of data. To process unbounded streams of data, we present a data flow langue, called Pig Latin Stream that is extended from Pig Latin. The Pig Latin Stream provides two window operators such as a record-based window operator and a time-based window operator as shown in Table 2. A window operator is a logical container for data recently received by an input source. So, window operators can handle data streams by using collection of data streams with a certain number or time. Pig Latin Stream also supports network-based IO interfaces for processing data streams as shown in Fig. 3. To read streams of data and write output sources, Pig Latin Stream provides LamaCepStorage function as load/store functions as shown in Fig. 3. The LamaCepStorage function of load operator provides two window types to process unbounded streams of structured text data. Store operator can use LamaCepStorage as a store function to store structured data streams on network or file on distributed stream processing systems. Pig Latin Stream supports window operators and network-based IO interfaces by adding specific functions like LamaCepStorage without changing the Pig Latin syntax provided in Pig system.

Table 2. Window operations on Pig Latin Stream.

	Record-based window	Time-based window
Concept	Emits collected records in defined certain number	Emits collected records in defined certain time
Syntax	LamaCepStorage('RecordWindow', 'size', 'sliding')	LamaCepStorage('TimeWindow', 'size', 'sliding')
Size	Size of window (number of records)	Size of window (millisecond)
Sliding	Size of sliding (number of records)	Size of sliding (millisecond)

```
Users = load 'tcp://192.168.10.11:9001' using LamaCepStorage('\t',
'TimeWindow', '3000', '1000')   as (name, age);

Pages = load 'file:///tmp/pages.txt' as (user, url);

FilterUsers = filter Users by age >= 20 and age <= 30;

JoinD = join FilterUsers by name, Pages by user;

GroupD = group JoinData by url;

ForeachD = foreach GroupD generate group,  COUNT(JoinD) as clicks;

OrderD = order ForeachD by clicks desc;

Top10 = limit OrderD 10;

store Top10 into 'tcp:///192.168.10.12:9002' using LamaCepStorage('|');
```

Fig. 3. An example of Pig Latin Stream

3.4   Compilation of Distributed Stream Processing Service

This section describes the process of translating Pig Latin Stream programs into distributed service jobs to be executed on distributed stream processing system. LAMA-CEP takes Pig Latin Stream programs as input sources and compiles them into distributed stream processing LAMA-SP service jobs jar and then submits the generated service jobs to LAMA-SP as shown in Fig. 4.

In the compilation, the basic operators of Pig Latin Stream are mapped into the tasks of LAMA-SP as shown in Fig. 5. For example, the load operator of Pig Latin Stream, which has a window function for processing streams of data, is mapped into the input task of LAMA-SP. The store operator of Pig Latin Stream also is mapped into

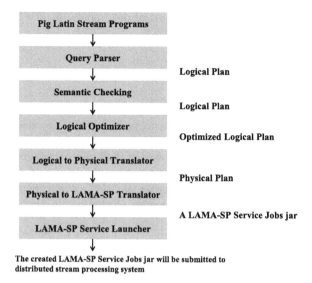

Fig. 4. The process of compilation of stream processing service jobs

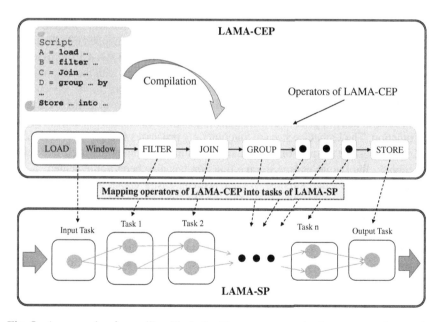

Fig. 5. An example of compiling Pig Latin Stream programs to stream processing service

the output task of LAMA-SP. Other basic relational operators (filter, join, group, etc.) are mapped into the general tasks of LAMA-SP in Fig. 5. That is to say, basic relational operators of Pig Latin Stream are executed as the tasks of LAMA-SP on a cluster of computes for processing unbounded streams of data rapidly by using distributed and parallel computing.

4 Implementation

LAMA-CEP system has been implemented by extending Pig system for supporting to process streams of data by adding the concept of window operators. The tasks of LAMA-CEP to be executed on distributed stream processing systems can be implemented by based on physical operators. However, if all of physical operators have their own classes of tasks in the implementation process, a lot of classes of LAMA-CEP's tasks may be needed. To reduce size of classes of tasks, we provide three type classes of LAMA-CEP's tasks based on the properties of relational operators. The tasks of LAMA-CEP are as follows:

- CepRecordTask: processes data by a tuple unit with single input source.
  ✓ Operators: filter, foreach, limit.
- CepSetTask: processes data by tuple set with single input source.
  ✓ Operators: distinct, rank, sort.
- CepMultiSetTask: processes data by tuple set with multi input sources.
  ✓ Operators: cogroup, cross, join, union

The three classes of LAMA-CEP's tasks should be inherited from the class interfaces of LAMA-SP because the tasks of LAMA-CEP should be mapped into the tasks of LAMA-SP and be executed on a LAMA-SP cluster system. LAMA-CEP provides the classes of LamaCepInout/LamaCepOutput that are implemented with the task objects of LamaInput/LamaOutput in LAMA-SP for load/store operators to be executed on LAMA-SP system. The LamaCepInout/LamaCepOutput classes in LAMA-CEP keep the functions of load/store such as a LamaCepStorage function and a LamaCepJsonStorage function. The LamaCepStorage function only processes streams of structured text data. To load or store streams of JSON data types that are commonly used like Twitter and Facebook, the LamaCepJsonStorage function has also been implemented.

To process unbounded streams of data, we can easily create a distributed stream processing service by using Pig Latin Stream data flow language, provided LAMA-CEP system. Figure 6 shows an example of real-time SNS analysis service. The functions of analysis service include real-time issue Twitter monitoring, issue word monitoring and reports. We can easily write Pig Latin Stream scripts with high-level data flow language in LAMA-CEP as shown in Fig. 6(a). The LAMA-CEP can generate LAMA-SP service jobs by compiling Pig Latin Stream programs. The tasks of generated LAMA-SP service jobs are executed on distributed computing nodes with Twitter data as input sources as shown in Fig. 6(b). If there is a crash in a certain physical node, the tasks that are executed in the crash node will be moved and executed to normal nodes again.

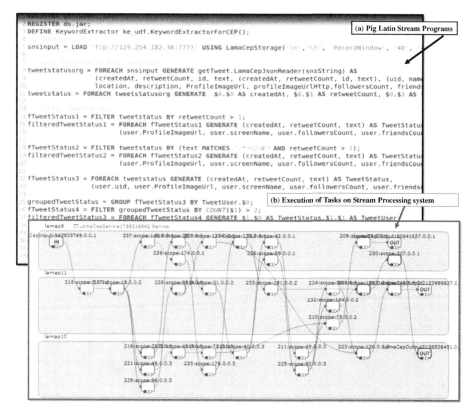

Fig. 6. An example of SNS analysis service on distributed stream processing systems

5 Conclusion

In this paper, we propose a data flow language processing system (LAMA-CEP), which supports to deploy services that continuously process huge streams of data in real-time. LAMA-CEP has been extended from Pig system to support stream data processing. To handle unbounded streams of data, we provide a data flow stream processing language (Pig Latin Stream) extended from Pig Latin by adding a window concept and network-based IO functions. Users can easily write service programs in using high-level data flow Pig Latin Stream language. LAMA-CEP translates stream processing services that are written in Pig Latin Stream language into DAG-based distributed stream processing service jobs to be executed on distributed stream processing system (LAMA-SP). Finally, the generated stream processing service jobs are submitted and executed on LAMA-SP to process large streams of data in real-time on a highly scalable distributed stream processing system.

Acknowledgments. This work was supported by the ICT R&D program of MSIP/IITP. [14-000-05-001, Smart Networking Core Technology Development].

References

1. Apache Hadoop. http://hadoop.apache.org/
2. Dean, J., Ghemawat, S.: MapReduce: simplified data processing on large clusters. Commun. ACM **51**(1), 107–113 (2008)
3. Apache Hadoop MapReduce. https://developer.yahoo.com/hadoop/tutorial/module4.html
4. Olston, C., Reed, B., Srivastava, U., Kumar, R., Tomkins, A.: Pig latin: a not-so-foreign language for data processing. In: Proceedings of the 2008 ACM SIGMOD International Conference on Management of Data, pp. 1099–1110, Vancouver, Canada (2008)
5. Apache Pig. http://hadoop.apache.org/pig/
6. Gantz, J.F.: The Diverse and Exploding Digital Universe. IDC (2008)
7. Distributed and fault-tolerant realtime computation. http://storm.incubator.apache.org/
8. Neumeyer, L., Robbins, B., Nair, A., Kesari, A.: S4: distributed stream computing platform. In: 10th IEEE International Conference on Data Mining Workshops (ICDMW), pp. 170–177, Sydney, Australia (2010)

Author Index